theatre & interculturalism

Ric Knowles

First published 2010 by
PALGRAVE MACMILLAN

Palgrave Macmillan in the UK is an imprint of Macmillan Publishers Limited, registered in England, company number 785998, of Houndmills, Basingstoke, Hampshire RG21 6XS.

Palgrave Macmillan in the US is a division of St Martin's Press LLC, 175 Fifth Avenue, New York, NY 10010.

Palgrave Macmillan is the global academic imprint of the above companies and has companies and representatives throughout the world.

Palgrave® and Macmillan® are registered trademarks in the United States, the United Kingdom, Europe and other countries.

ISBN 978–0–230–57548–6   paperback

This book is printed on paper suitable for recycling and made from fully managed and sustained forest sources. Logging, pulping and manufacturing processes are expected to conform to the environmental regulations of the country of origin.

A catalogue record for this book is available from the British Library.

A catalog record for this book is available from the Library of Congress.

Printed and bound in China

contents

For Christine

The theatre is everywhere, from entertainment districts to the fringes, from the rituals of government to the ceremony of the courtroom, from the spectacle of the sporting arena to the theatres of war. Across these many forms stretches a theatrical continuum through which cultures both assert and question themselves.

Theatre has been around for thousands of years, and the ways we study it have changed decisively. It's no longer enough to limit our attention to the canon of Western dramatic literature. Theatre has taken its place within a broad spectrum of performance, connecting it with the wider forces of ritual and revolt that thread through so many spheres of human culture. In turn, this has helped make connections across disciplines; over the past fifty years, theatre and performance have been deployed as key metaphors and practices with which to rethink gender, economics, war, language, the fine arts, culture and one's sense of self.

Theatre & is a long series of short books which hopes to capture the restless interdisciplinary energy of theatre and performance. Each book explores connections between theatre and some aspect of the wider world, asking how the theatre might illuminate the world and how the world might illuminate the theatre. Each book is written by a leading theatre scholar and represents the cutting edge of critical thinking in the discipline.

We have been mindful, however, that the philosophical and theoretical complexity of much contemporary academic writing can act as a barrier to a wider readership. A key aim for these books is that they should all be readable in one sitting by anyone with a curiosity about the subject. The books are challenging, pugnacious, visionary sometimes and, above all, clear. We hope you enjoy them.

Jen Harvie and Dan Rebellato

theatre & interculturalism

This book concerns itself with theatrical attempts to bridge cultures through performance, to bring different cultures into productive dialogue with one another on the stage, in the space between the stage and the audience, and within the audience. It begins with the assumption that culture – the fluid, day-to-day, lived realities of specific peoples in specific places and at specific times – exists only insofar as it is enacted, performed into being by the daily and (extra-daily) ritual and performative activities of individuals and communities as they negotiate their place in the world. Its focus is on how cultures and cultural forms interact and negotiate their differences through performative exchange and on the relationships between theatre and performance, interculturalism, and the formation of individual and community identities in an increasingly multicultural world. But this is fraught territory, and it raises issues about cultural imperialism, appropriation, and colonisation, even

1

as it offers the utopian promise of a world where race and cultural difference do not matter.

Part of what is fraught in this enterprise is a history of interculturalism and its criticism that is firmly located in the west, where the resources and reasons to dominate exchange are concentrated. That history is reflected in this book. As a complex and multiple kind of intercultural performance emerges internationally outside, or in negotiation with, the containments of traditional western theatre, pressure is exerted to address intercultural performance in newly complex ways and to accommodate the fact of its newly diverse audiences. But the critical discourse, so far, remains firmly grounded in the western academy. Although I am attempting to address emerging developments and suggest fresh approaches in intercultural practice, particularly within newly global cities, it is that discourse that is my primary subject.

Theatrical interculturalism and its discontents

What *is* 'interculturalism'? The term is contested. Some view it with suspicion, seeing it, as Daryl Chin does in 'Interculturalism, Postmodernism, Pluralism', as a debased, contemporary form of cultural imperialism (1991, p. 94), or even, as Una Chaudhuri suggests in 'The Future of the Hyphen', as 'cultural rape' (1991, p. 193). Others, notably its chief western practitioners, such as Peter Brook, see the potential for intercultural performance to produce a utopia by putting performers from a variety of cultural backgrounds together in search of a common humanity. Others still, such as Christopher Murray, in Lizbeth Goodman and Jane de

Gay's *Routledge Reader in Politics and Performance*, fear that the idea of genuinely intercultural theatre is a chimera or, worse, 'a (Trojan?) horse designed by a committee' (2000, p. 89) – a charge that used to be directed against theatrical collectives, including those feminist collectives that Goodman, among others, has elsewhere championed. Clearly, as Chin says, 'to deploy elements from the symbolic system of another culture is a very delicate enterprise' (p. 94).

Nevertheless, interculturalism is an urgent topic in the twenty-first century. As cities and nations move beyond the monochromatic, as human traffic between nations and cultures (both willing and unwilling) increases, as hybridity and syncretism (the merging of forms) become increasingly characteristic of cultural production everywhere, and as nineteenth-century nationalism gives way to twenty-first century *trans*nationalism, it becomes imperative that the ways in which cultural exchange is performed be critically re-examined. *Theatre & Interculturalism* is designed to perform such a re-examination. In addition to providing a critical survey of historical and contemporary approaches to the topic, it aims to propose new ways of thinking about theatrical flow across cultures and the ways in which human subjectivity and identity are constituted – brought into being – through performance.

For the purpose, I am defining both terms of my title broadly. In the interests of not privileging contemporary western formulations, I consider 'theatre' to refer to all cultural forms in which performers and active or passive participant-audiences coexist in the same space for a set time. I also frequently use 'performance' throughout this book to refer to practices that are explicitly concerned with the performative (that is, formative) constitution of identities or subjectivities through ritual, habitual, or self-conscious behaviours that occur outside the formal framing of 'theatre' as a western art form. I prefer 'intercultural' to the other terms available — cross-cultural, extracultural, intracultural, metacultural, multicultural, precultural, postcultural, transcultural, transnational, ultracultural, and so on — because it seems to me important to focus on the contested, unsettling, and often unequal spaces *between* cultures, spaces that can function in performance as sites of negotiation. Unlike 'cross-cultural', 'intercultural' evokes the possibility of interaction across a multiplicity of cultural positionings, avoiding binary codings. This means, too, that I prefer some forms of theatrical practice and theory over others, and I exclude some work, albeit intriguing for other reasons, from consideration altogether. This exclusion includes work such as the random postmodern collages of the artists Bernard-Marie Koltès, Heiner Müller, and Robert Wilson, which are often treated under the sign of intercultural performance but which don't invoke concomitant larger cultural *discourses* where cultural exchange can effectively occur and new hybrid identities can emerge.

In *Women's Intercultural Performance*, Julie Holledge and Joanne Tompkins define theatrical interculturalism as 'the meeting in the moment of performance of two or more cultural traditions' (2000, p. 7), and this seems as clear a definition as any. Intercultural theatre and performance, then, I understand to be a site for the continuing renegotiation

4

of cultural values and the reconstitution of individual and community identities and subject positions.

As such, theatrical interculturalism raises a number of questions about what Joseph Roach calls, in the first edition of *Critical Theory and Performance*, 'the feasibility of theatre as a mediator across boundaries of historical and cultural difference' (1996, p. 13). Erika Fischer-Lichte lists some of these questions in 'Theatre, Own and Foreign':

> [D]oes interculturalism have a completely spe-
> cific function in each culture to fulfil, or can
> one locate general aims and goals which serve as
> worldwide phenomena? Does interculturalism
> in theatre indicate national, continental or world
> culture? Does it guarantee and confirm cultural
> identity, or does it metamorphose or even dis-
> solve identity? Is it a question of the attempt to
> propagate an awareness of a foreign culture, or
> is it rather a cultural exploitation? Does theat-
> rical interculturalism today support and provoke
> intercultural understanding, or does it deny
> fundamental differences between cultures and
> make any communication impossible, if one is
> deceived into believing in a shared community,
> which actually does not exist? (1990, p. 18)

In addition to these questions, I ask in this book about inter-sections between intercultural performance studies and other critical approaches – performance studies, critical

multiculturalism studies, critical race theory and critical whiteness studies, diaspora studies, and critical cosmopolitanism.
I ask how intercultural performance functions if approached
'from below' rather than from the position of privilege, how
the stage can be decolonised, and how inequities in the cultural mix can be dissolved and solidarities forged across difference. And I ask about the intercultural performance ecology
of the twenty-first-century city. But first, I ask what it would
mean to broaden the historical scope of intercultural performance studies beyond the past hundred years or so.

Theatre has always been intercultural

Intercultural performance is not new, though its wide-
spread, conscious practice in the western world began only
in the twentieth century, and its theorisation in the western
academy in the 1970s and 1980s. For thousands of years
the Indigenous peoples of the world negotiated difference
and facilitated trade in part through performance forms –
the potlatch among the peoples of the northwest coast of
what is now North America, the Koha among the Māori,
the kula ring in the Kiriwina (Trobriand) Islands and the
Moka and Sepik Coast exchanges in Papua New Guinea's
western highlands and northern coastal areas, respectively.
(With very different intents and purposes, Indigenous performance continues to be trotted out today in the opening
ceremonies of international sporting events and festivals to
shore up latter-day visions of national authenticity.)

In Africa, in Australia, in New Zealand, pre-contact,
pre-capitalist cultures tended to be fluid, 'open-minded,

ready to draw on the foreign as a source of unfolding, re-shaping, strengthening', as Joachim Fiebach argues of the African Yoruba people in his contribution to Fischer-Lichte et al.'s 1990 collection *The Dramatic Touch of Difference* (p. 270). In *Performance and Cosmopolitics*, Helen Gilbert and Jacqueline Lo describe a contemporary use of this history by the Gungalidda elder Wadjularbinna, who challenged John Howard's efforts as Australian prime minister to restrict entry to the country by asylum seekers (refugees) and 'boat people', on the basis of what Gilbert and Lo call 'an autochthonous [Indigenous] form of cosmopolitanism'. Howard and the rest of the non-Indigenous establishment, Wadjularbinna argued, are themselves descended from 'boat people' and are only in Australia through the (violated) generosity of Aboriginal kinship systems and their belief that 'people can come here, if they respect our land, and treat our land as it should be treated [...] and if they respect our differences' (2007, pp. 207–8). In New Zealand, according to Māori writer and performer Roma Potiki, the Māori *marae* is at once a meeting house (where culture is negotiated) and a theatre: 'and we have had this theatre for hundreds of years' ('It Is Political If It Can Be Passed On', 1996, p. 173). Christopher Balme, in his essay 'Between Separation and Integration', describes *marae* rituals such as the *whaikōrero* as 'a balanced [intercultural] exchange between locals (*tangata whenua*) and visitors (*manuhiri*)' (1996, p. 182).

China, Japan, Korea, and India also have traditions of intercultural performance that date back hundreds of years. In his contribution to *The Dramatic Touch of Difference*

James R. Brandon describes how during the Nara period (646–749) the Japanese exchanged performance traditions with China and Korea, so the *bugaku* court dance and the Buddhist processional dance-play, *gugaku*, were introduced into Japan and eventually became part of Japanese culture (1990, p. 89). The famous *kathakali* drama from the state of Kerala in India was derived in the seventeenth century from a mix of performance traditions that included the Sanskrit dance-drama the *kutiyattam*, itself, since 2001, a UNESCO-protected cultural expression and one that dates back two millennia. Ironically, the prefix *kuti-*, in the Malayalam language of Kerala, means 'mixed', and *attam* means 'acting'; this oldest of classical forms, then, is explicitly rooted in a mixture of ancient performance styles.

From the sixteenth to the twenty-first century, much of the interculturalism in eastern Asia, as among the world's Indigenous peoples, derived from 'negotiations' (on unequal terms) with western forms. Sixteenth- and seventeenth-century Japan briefly dallied with European (mostly Portuguese and Dutch) cultural production, principally in the form of trade, but the long-term impact of western theatre on Japanese performance forms was negligible until American and European invasions in the late nineteenth century.

Beginning at the turn of the twentieth century and lasting almost a hundred years, the *shingeki* (new drama) movement saw a turn in Japan to Shakespeare, Ibsen, Chekhov, Stanislavski, and the performance styles of western naturalism and spoken drama. In the first decade of the twentieth century, in the wake of China's defeat in the Sino-Japanese war of 1894–5, a similar movement developed in China, largely through the conscious efforts of Li Xishuang and Tokyo's Spring Willow society, and visits to the society by Chinese students who produced the first *huaju* (spoken drama) – including an adaptation of the American novel-turned-play *Uncle Tom's Cabin* at Hongo-za theatre in Tokyo in 1907. According to Fischer-Lichte in 'Theatre, Own and Foreign', the Friends of the New Theatre opened its own Spring Willow Theatre in Shanghai in 1914, just as war, modernism, and the avant-garde were breaking out in Europe (p. 14), and the west's wholesale consumption of 'oriental' forms began in earnest.

Meanwhile in Africa and India in the early twentieth century, theatrical interculturalism developed primarily in response to, and as a result of, colonisation. Thus in Africa in the 1920s, local content was contained within North American minstrel, English music hall, and Hollywood imitations, particularly within concert parties in Ghana, which were nevertheless consistently anti-colonialist in content. In Nigeria, the Yoruba travelling theatre, created out of a missionary Christian choral tradition in the 1930s, came to integrate traditional Yoruban movement, arts, ceremonies, and legends and had a significant role in affirming the cultural identity of the Yoruba people, to the degree that Yoruba culture now tends to dominate discourses of Nigerian theatre, suggesting an internal cultural hegemony in relation to the four hundred and fifty language and cultural groupings within only one of fifty-two African countries. Indian theatre in the same period initially mimicked

British forms (in Homi Bhabha's sense of colonial mimicry in *The Location of Culture* – '*almost the same, but not white*', 1994, p. 89, emphasis in original). The Parsi theatre copied nineteenth-century English staging practices but incorporated classical Indian dance and music, drawing themes from Parsi romances and Hindu mythology. Despite the mimicry of British formal properties, much of this work was, again, explicitly anti-colonialist in content.

The function of the integration of forms across cultures during this period is clearly site-specific and varies significantly from culture to culture (which, as African and Indian examples make clear, does not coincide with either nation or continent). All this varies according to local configurations of power. But according to Richard Schechner in his 1996 essay 'Interculturalism and the Culture of Choice', the blending of western and Indigenous forms in colonised or dominated cultures often constituted an attempt 'to find out what it was that they found of value in Western societies; that is, what they could use in their struggle for independence against Western national domination' (p. 43). In the west, however, intercultural performance since the sixteenth century has served very different purposes and taken very different forms.

It can be argued that western theatrical forms, like performance forms elsewhere, have always been hybrid. Standard theatre histories trace the birth of western theatre to the sixth-century BCE festival of Dionysus in ancient Greece, but the ritual forms and mythological figures upon which that festival was built were probably Middle Eastern or African in origin. Roman drama, itself a hybrid founded on a misunderstood Greek model, mixed with sixteenth-century Italian commedia dell'arte, French and Italian romance, and Anglo-Celtic folk traditions to produce the blend that was Elizabethan comedy. Molière included 'Turkish' scenes in his seventeenth-century comedies, and Voltaire 'Chinese' ones in the eighteenth century. But according to Fischer-Lichte's essay 'Interculturalism in Contemporary Theatre' (1996, pp. 28–9), interculturalism became 'a conscious program' only with Goethe's work at the Weimar Theatre in Germany (1791–1817) – where he nevertheless produced only plays from the European canon – and in his own masterpiece, *Faust*, which was deeply influenced by Sanskrit drama. At Weimar Goethe began a long tradition in the west of using intercultural links to access 'truths' that were supposed to be universal.

But the heyday of interculturalism in the west – at least insofar as it involved contact or integration with, or appropriation of, the cultural forms of the 'other' (Indigenous, 'oriental', or other non-western peoples) – began with the European modernist movement at the turn of the twentieth century, and this is the period with which most histories of intercultural performance begin. The early decades of the twentieth century witnessed a rash of 'discoveries' on the part of western theatre practitioners, as these artists scoured the world's performance cultures in an effort to revitalise and renew a decadent western tradition. Thus William Butler Yeats, Jacques Copeau, a nd many others turned for inspiration to Japanese *nō* d rama; Edward Gordon Craig discovered African masks (though he feared and revered the 'mysteries' of the 'Holy East', keeping his distance from it); Max Reinhardt turned to the Japanese *hanamichi* (the flower path linking stage to auditorium) in his attempt to reconfigure proscenium stagecraft; and Vsevolod Meyerhold became intrigued with non-realist Japanese modes of representation. These 'discoveries' shored up very different theatrical visions and programmes, and these artists had varying degrees of respect for their chosen other cultures (and for difference more generally). But most of the modernist theatre that resulted involved the incorporation of elements of the performance forms or techniques of non-European cultures in ways that removed them from their social contexts, histories, and belief systems, othering them, treating them as exotica, or reducing them to their purely formal or aesthetic properties. It was in this cannibalisation of forms without respect for the cultures that produced them that early interculturalism most directly participated in the west's colonisation of the world's cultures and peoples.

Of these 'discoveries', the most influential in terms of the theory and practice of interculturalism in the twentieth century and beyond have been Antonin Artaud's encounter with Balinese dance at the Paris Colonial Exposition in 1931 and Bertolt Brecht's discovery of Chinese acting in a performance in Moscow in 1935 by leading actor Mei Lanfang. Artaud's discovery led directly to the formulation of his 'theatre of cruelty' in his essay 'On the Balinese Theater', first published in 1931; Brecht's to his first use of the term *Verfremdungseffekt* ('defamiliarization effect') in his 1936 essay 'Alienation Effects in Chinese Acting', upon which much of his subsequent work was built. These two figures, as theoreticians and practitioners, were the progenitors of two distinct streams of western theatrical interculturalism that dominated theatrical practice and theory in the western world throughout the twentieth century. I call these streams universalist (or idealist) and materialist. Richard Schechner, in his 2002 book *Performance Studies: An Introduction*, makes a parallel distinction between the 'integrative' and 'disruptive' strands of intercultural performance (p. 251), and Lo and Gilbert, in 'Toward a Topography of Cross-Cultural Theatre Practice', talk similarly about the political and the aesthetic (2002, p. 43).

Brecht and the materialists

Like Artaud with Balinese theatre, as we will see in the next section, Brecht found what he was looking for when he discovered Chinese acting; like Artaud's, his subsequent work was deeply informed by that discovery; and like Artaud's, his work has been monumentally influential. Unlike Artaud, however, Brecht was committed not to avant-garde art or to individual psychology but to the political potential of theatre to change the world. And unlike Artaud's, his influence has not been limited to the west. His was not a search for the transcendent in some mysterious east; rather, he was looking for a model for his own, non-psychological, non-Aristotelian 'epic theatre', one that did not, as in the Aristotelian model, rely for its effects on empathy and catharsis (the purging of pity and fear) but kept its audience focused on the realm of the social and historical. His admiration for Chinese acting has to do with the performer's never becoming lost in the emotion that she or he represents. Indeed, when Brecht admires the fact that there is 'nothing eruptive' about the Chinese artist's representation of passion (1964, p. 93) he could be writing a critique of Artaud's theatre of cruelty, to which the eruption of 'primitive' passion is central. Because Brecht wanted above all to bring the audience to see and understand the nature of social reality he theorised an acting style derived from what he understood to be a complex layering in Chinese theatre, where he felt that actors limited themselves 'to simply *quoting* the character played' (p. 94, emphasis added) and representing each incident 'as a unique, historical one' (p. 98) rather than an example of a universal (and therefore inevitable, unchangeable) truth.

Brecht influenced the history of western theatre to the point that 'the alienation effect' has been co-opted as a now familiar, decorative feature in the very kinds of bourgeois theatre he despised – as mere effect. But Brecht has also been a major influence on materialist theory and criticism – criticism that grounds itself in material realities rather than platonic ideals, in the realms of the social and historical rather than the psychological and universal. This includes the types of intercultural theory developed by critics such as Rustom Bharucha, Biodun Jeyifo, Christopher Balme, Julie Holledge and Joanne Tompkins, Jacqueline Lo and Helen Gilbert, examined in this book. It is also striking that Brecht's own theatrical work, inspired by his appropriation of Chinese acting, has been reappropriated in such places as Japan, Africa, India, and China itself, as is demonstrated consistently throughout Fischer-Lichte et al.'s *The Dramatic*

Touch of Difference. There Iwabuchi Tatsuji writes about the complexities of Brecht's divided reception in Japan; Vasudha Dalmia-Lüderitz, in an essay titled 'To Be More Brechtian Is to Be More Indian', deals in detail with the use of Brecht by the great Hindi playwright Habib Tanvir; and Ola Rotimi, in an essay entitled 'Much Ado about Brecht', compares epic theatre with traditional African practice. Rotimi wryly points out that Brecht 'extracted some raw materials from the matrix of Third World theatre' only to have them now 'packaged and labelled and exported anew into the Third World' (p. 259).

But to return to China: in the same volume, in an essay entitled 'On the Insatiable Appetite and Longevity of Theatre', Ding Yangzhong describes Brecht as 'probably the most significant foreign, modern dramatist' in China (p. 170), and he provides an account of his own adaptation of *The Good Person of Sezuan* in the style of Sichuan song-dance theatre, performed at the first China-Brecht symposium in Beijing in 1985. Noting Brecht's borrowings from Chinese theatre, Ding sees this intercultural reappropriation as 'reaping the interest on our loan' (p. 171). And Ding was not alone. Many major Chinese theatre artists, including Sun Huizhu, Sha Yexin, He Zishuang, Wang Peigong, Ma Zhongjun, and, notably, Nobel Prize-winner Gao Xingjian, have since the 1980s been involved in the reimportation and reinterpretation of Brecht. Gao's *Wild Man*, also staged in Beijing in 1985 (People's Art Theatre), used a cast of dozens of actors, singers, and musicians to deal dialectically with the ecological effects of rapid industrialisation in an effective reinvention and reappropriation of Brecht that, unlike most absorptions of Brechtian techniques in contemporary western theatre, also revived Brecht's political purposes.

Artaud and his doubles: the universalists

Like Brecht, Artaud was a staunch opponent of the bourgeois theatre, but he was no materialist. And although he returned to his essay on the Balinese theatre throughout his life, continually fine-tuning it, Artaud did not stop with the Balinese in his raiding of other cultures. In *Theatre and the World* Rustom Bharucha has described Artaud's 'eclectic, almost frantic need to absorb non-western cultures [...] decontextualiz[ing] their realities within the incandescence of his vision' (1993, p. 14). Indeed, Artaud was less interested in the specificities of the other than its very otherness, as what Bharucha calls 'a stimulus for his dreams' about an 'oriental theatre' of his own invention (p. 15). Artaud's oriental theatre never existed; nevertheless, his writings made it real for a charismatic (European, male) lineage that includes Jerzy Grotowski, Eugenio Barba, Peter Brook, and others who focus most intensely on the art of the actor and who can be loosely grouped as 'the universalists'.

Artaud is better known for his theory than for his practice, and among his writings his best-known book is *The Theatre and Its Double* (English translation 1958), in which he articulates his ideas about a plague-like 'theatre of cruelty' that would break through language and touch life, the secret forces of the universe, and the transcendent impulses of the deepest self. He valued oriental theatre primarily because it eschewed naturalism and, seen from his outsider's point of view at least, approached the intensity and frenzy of (primitive) ritual – though he failed to recognise the trained precision of its technique and the precise signification of its gestural vocabulary. It is this faith in the primitive, in something that precedes language and culture, something elementally human, that links Artaud to Grotowski, Barba, and Brook, in their various ways, and explains their interculturalism.

From the start of his career in the 1960s, Polish theatre guru Jerzy Grotowski worked diachronically (through history) to connect with 'other' cultures, studying yoga, Chinese philosophy, and world religions and introducing these studies into his work with actors. During his 'Objective Drama' project in the mid-1980s in California his focus was on finding specific elements in the work of performers from around the globe that *transcended* their own cultures; he believed that the deeper one investigated the essential self, anywhere, the more likely one was to find the archetypal – which he called the 'objective' – bases for ritual, and therefore theatre. His attention to the specifics of particular cultural forms of classical Chinese theatre and Indian *kathakali*, and his efforts to demystify them by finding their essences, differentiates him radically from Artaud. But as with Artaud, Grotowski's search was for origins and for ahistorical essences. For him, 'man precedes difference', as Bonnie Marranca observes in her introductory essay to *Interculturalism and Performance* (1991, p. 16), and in his essay 'Performer', Grotowski states that 'essence interests me because nothing in it is sociological' (1997, p. 377), making explicit his divergence from Brecht. Ultimately, Grotowski's search was for what he considered to be the deep psychophysical sources of performance.

Eugenio Barba was Grotowski's student, disciple, and assistant for three years in the early 1960s, and it was Barba who introduced Grotowski to *kathakali*. Barba has been a major figure in the theory and practice of interculturalism through his work in Denmark at the Odin Teatret and at the International School of Theatre Anthropology, which he founded in 1979, and through his publications and those of his followers and collaborators. Like Grotowski, Barba is interested in the 'pre-' (what precedes performance itself, or any other type of expression), though unlike his mentor he tends to work synchronically across contemporary cultures rather than diachronically across historical or ancient ones. Nevertheless, much of Barba's work can be seen as an extension of Grotowski's investigations into the source of the actor's power, energy, and presence. Working with an international, intercultural team of performers, and focusing much of his attention on Asian performance training, Barba searches for universals in what he calls the 'pre-expressive': movements, rhythms, and stances that recur in the trained, extra-ordinary bodies of performers across cultures. In his somewhat idiosyncratic 'Theatre Anthropology', Barba asserts the existence of a transcultural physiology that precedes conscious expression (or culture) in bodies that are honed and ready through exhaustive training regimes (see Barba and Savarese, *A Dictionary of Theatre Anthropology*, 1991).

Barba's downfall is like Grotowski's: he is determinedly ahistorical, removing elements of performance from the social, cultural, and theatrical or ritual contexts that produced them and where they produce their meanings. He privileges (select-ive examples of) sameness – patterns that can be understood to be shared across differences that can themselves be under-stood to be accidental, or 'merely cultural', rather than of the essence. As with many universalisms or essentialisms, the problem with this is that what is 'of the essence' can too easily be identified with what is culturally dominant, particularly under the leadership of a powerful and charismatic western director such as Barba. Nevertheless, Barba has made import-ant contributions to theorising the intercultural through his concept of a 'third theatre' and his practice of performative barter. Barba's third theatre is articulated as different from a 'first', institutionalised and subsidised, theatre of entertain-ment and a 'second', avant-garde, theatre of aesthetic experi-mentation and novelty through its focus on the production of meaning (or the semiotic). The third theatre also makes claims to a kind of marginalisation, as signalled through the hom-ology with 'third world', or even with Homi Bhabha's 'Third Space' between global and national cultures (*The Location of Culture*, 1994, p. 37), even if this parallel is not in mater-ial terms earned: Barba is well funded, well respected, and culturally privileged. But as Barba argues in *A Dictionary of Theatre Anthropology*, 'the character of the Third Theatre is the autonomous construction of meaning which does not recognise the boundaries assigned to our craft by the sur-rounding culture' (p. 8). Despite the enabling fiction (or falsehood) that meaning can be produced in isolation from the surrounding culture, this means that his focus is less on a theatrical product than on the process of meaning-making itself. His focus is on specific people from different cultures working together and on what he calls 'barter': the meeting of cultures in exchanges of performances, in which the value of the work rests not in the product but in the exchange itself. This model, however, disregards material inequalities, power and funding differentials, and the different ways in which performances are situated within cultures, all of which, without the proverbial level playing field, make very fragile the possibility of genuine intercultural exchange. The first peoples of the Americas also thought they were engaging in barter when they exchanged the lands that they inhabited (but never claimed to own) for a few beads, alcohol, gunpowder, and smallpox.

Perhaps chief among the universalists, and the one who brought Artaud's theatre of cruelty to prominence with a season devoted to it by the Royal Shakespeare Company in London in 1964, is Peter Brook. Four years after that season, and very much under the influence of Grotowski and his concept of 'poor theatre' (focusing not on spectacle but on the actor's encounter with the spectator), Brook articulated the basis of his universalism at the outset of his widely influential book *The Empty Space*: 'I can take any empty space and call it a bare stage. A man walks across this empty space whilst someone else is watching him, and this is all I need for an act of theatre to be engaged' ([1968] 1979, p. 11). Key to understanding this passage in relation to Brook's later intercultural work at the Centre international de création théâtrale (which he founded in Paris in 1971 with funding from the Ford Foundation, UNESCO, and other sources) is Brook's faith in his own power and capacity ('I can take', 'all I need') to constitute a space as 'empty' – free of the social and cultural predeterminants, inequities, and power relationships that are constitutive of culture and ideology. But ideology abhors a vacuum, and there is no such thing as an empty space. And this, together with Brook's assumption of power and ownership, is at the heart of what I think of as the 'interculture wars' that were provoked in large part by Brook's nine-hour 1985 production (Festival d'Avignon) and four-year world tour of *The Mahabharata*, adapted for the stage by Brook and Jean-Claude Carrière from the great Sanskrit epic of ancient India, a major sacred text for Hindus.

The west and the rest

The Mahabharata, along with the mid-1980s work of French director Ariane Mnouchkine (particularly her *Les Shakespeares* cycle, 1981–4; *Sihanouk*, 1985; and *L'Indiade*, 1987–8, all at Théâtre du soleil at Le Cartoucherie, Paris), was a crucible for the developing discourses of theatrical interculturalism. The productions themselves, and more notably their divided reception, threw into relief the tendency of intercultural theatre and its scholarship to split the world into a 'west and the rest' binary that was both fundamental and problematic. The reception of these shows, particularly of *The Mahabharata* by Indian scholars, exposed the degree to which the discourses of intercultural performance – beginning with the work of Richard Schechner and Victor Turner on the anthropology of performance – had been overwhelmingly dominated by white westerners, mostly charismatic men. As such, intercultural performance had unwittingly participated in the commodification of the 'other' and thereby the perpetuation of the colonial project, in which the raw materials of the world (including its cultures and peoples) were and are grist for the colonial mill of western industry and capitalist production.

The Mahabharata was not Brook's first foray into 'othered' cultures. Indeed, the core purpose of his Centre international, where he gathered an international group of senior artists, was to investigate world performance cultures in search of a universal theatrical language. This was taken quite literally in the case of *Orghast* (1971), written by poet Ted Hughes in an invented 'universal' language. Hughes's orghast attempted to operate linguistically at a 'pre-rational' level, and Brook's *Orghast* was performed – characteristically for Brook, who prefers resonant spaces that evoke transhistorical continuities – in the ruins of the ancient Persian city of Persepolis. During 1972–4 the Centre international group travelled across Saharan Africa exchanging performances, searching out ancient rituals. Ultimately out of this experience and through residencies at El Teatro Campesino in California, a Chipewa reservation in Minnesota, and the Brooklyn Academy of Music, they produced *The Conference of the Birds* (Festival d'Avignon, 1979), based on a long twelfth-century poem by the Sufi mystic Farid ud-Din Attar. In 1975 they produced *The Ik*

(Les Bouffes du Nord, Paris), based on a book by Colin Turnbull about the Teuso, or Ik, peoples of northeastern Uganda. But *The Mahabharata* was perhaps Brook's most ambitious piece, with performers cast from nineteen nations, and its years of extensive international touring subjected his principles to scrutiny, and critique, that they had rarely experienced previously.

Chief among Brook's critics were Rustom Bharucha, Una Chaudhuri, Gautam Dasgupta, Biodun Jeyifo, and Jacqueline Lo and Helen Gilbert – and not incidentally, most of these scholars were writing from non-western subject positions and reintroducing materialist critique into the discourses of interculturalism. Among his supporters, mostly European, were Patrice Pavis, Erika Fischer-Lichte, and David Williams. Jeyifo critiques Brook's treatment of Africa as a blank slate; Dasgupta points to *The Mahabharata*'s exoticising orientalism and its distortions of a sacred text; Chaudhuri critiques its decontextualising displacements of material from India into a western performance context; and Lo and Gilbert, in their article 'Toward a Topography of Cross-Cultural Practice', criticise it for 'stripp[ing] the readable signs of culture from the source text rather than provok[ing] the audience to examine the tensions between participating cultures' (p. 47).

But Bharucha was Brook's principal antagonist in the interculture wars. In *Theatre and the World*, Bharucha calls *The Mahabharata* 'one of the most blatant (and accomplished) appropriations in recent years', and he provides a 'view from India' that is quite damning of Brook's enterprise as

analogous to that of the British Raj, calling it the 'appropriation and reordering of non-western material within an
orientalist framework of thought and action, which has been
specifically designed for the international market' (p. 68).
Bharucha's critique includes the important observation that,
although Brook gathers together actors from an impressive
number and range of cultures, they work in English, and
under the total control of Brook himself: 'once he places his
mark on his materials, they no longer belong to their cultures. They become part of his world' (p. 81). Bharucha's
argument is lengthy and detailed, but at heart it represents
a fundamentally materialist critique from the position of
a colonised culture of Brook's unwaveringly appropriative
and idealist universalism: 'one cannot separate the culture
from the text' (p. 70) – or the performance.

The Mahabharata has also, of course, been widely
admired, particularly in the west, and along with the
much more carefully situated and contextualized work of
Mnouchkine has been celebrated as successful interculturalism. Brook himself has outlined his deeply humanist
programme eloquently, particularly in his autobiographical book The Shifting Point (1987), moving many readers
profoundly with his idealist vision of the superficiality of
cultural difference and the universality of primal human
experience. Marvin Carlson, in his 1990 essay 'Peter Brook's
"The Mahabharata" and Ariane Mnouchkine's "L'Indiade" as
Examples of Contemporary Cross-Cultural Theatre', char-
acterises Brook's project not as intercultural but as transcultural, citing Brook's goal of imagining into being those

things that unite all cultures, and linking his work with that of Artaud (p. 54). But chief among the scholarly apologists for Brook, and for Mnouchkine, has been Patrice Pavis, who places the work of these two European artists, specifically *The Mahabharata* and *L'Indiade*, at the centre of his 1990 essay 'Interculturalism in Contemporary Mise en Scène'. There Pavis makes one of the earliest attempts to 'imagine', as he says, 'a theoretical model that would describe [...] the way in which the mise en scène presents and transmits a foreign culture to the public' (p. 57). Pavis finds in Brook and Mnouchkine different models for an intercultural theatre that in different ways successfully communicates 'an aspect of the mythical and historical India' to a western audience (p. 57) – a project that, in its unidirectionality, does not sound terribly *inter*cultural.

What is centrally problematic about Pavis's efforts is that they focus on the responsibility of the western artist to control the circumstances of the (intercultural) exchange: 'He [*sic*] must [...] arrange the source culture's reception and predict those arrangements that will facilitate communication between cultures' (p. 66). In this model, Brook is praised for moving *The Mahabharata* closer to a western audience; that is, he is praised for exactly those adaptations – or distortions – of sacred Hindu forms and narratives that Bharucha and others have critiqued. In focusing on 'readability' and 'reception within the target culture' of western audiences (p. 67), Pavis is fully prepared to sacrifice accuracy to the specificities of, or resonances within, the source cultures, in exchange for legibility or acceptance 'at home'. And for Pavis and others, 'at home' is the presumably monocultural west.

Most significant about Pavis's analysis for my purposes are the binaries it establishes. His famous 'hourglass' model of intercultural exchange, first articulated in this essay and elaborated in his 1992 book *Theatre at the Crossroads of Culture* (pp. 4–6), set the terms for a debate in the 1990s that circulated around the explicitly appropriative relationship between source and target cultures, most often articulated by Pavis as 'our culture and that of others' (p. 5). Pavis's hourglass model posits a one-way flow and filtering of information from source to target culture rather than any kind of fluid interchange. For Fischer-Lichte and her co-editors, awkwardly, but trying to be flexible about who 'us' might be understood to be, 'intercultural performance [...] is constituted by the relationship between the continuation of the own traditions [by which she means those of the target, or host, culture] and the productive reception of elements of foreign theatre traditions' (Preface to *The Dramatic Touch of Difference*, 1990, p. 5). Marvin Carlson, too, in his 1996 essay 'Brook and Mnouchkine', carefully maps out seven stages in the relationship between 'the culturally familiar and the culturally foreign' (pp. 82–3) that nevertheless perpetuate the binary. Even Jacqueline Lo and Helen Gilbert, in their critique of the unidirectionality of Pavis's hourglass model in 'Toward a Topography of Cross-Cultural Praxis', replace it with a new model allowing for traffic in both directions between what nevertheless remain two (and only two) cultures (p. 45).

The clearest crystallisation of the binary, and the clearest manifestation of its impact, comes with Pavis's widely read 1996 collection *The Intercultural Performance Reader*, where the Hegelian 'dialectic' that Pavis refers to in *Theatre at the Crossroads of Culture* (p. 2) manifests itself in the book's structure. After an introduction by Pavis and a section on 'Historical Contexts' that allows Pavis through Fischer-Lichte, Richard Schechner, and Josette Féral to frame the history of intercultural performance as western, the book is divided into three sections. The 'thesis' section, entitled 'Intercultural Performance from the Western Point of View', includes essays by and about Brook and Mnouchkine and largely celebrates the work of western interculturalists. The 'antithesis', entitled 'Intercultural Performance from Another Point of View', provides critiques from several 'other' points of view, including Africa (Jeyifo), India (Bharucha), New Zealand (Balme), and Chinese America (William Sun and Fae Fei). It also includes 'contextualising' introductions by Pavis that tend, in the framework of the book as a whole, to undercut the 'other' positions represented. (Pavis anxiously returns throughout the volume to diatribes against 'the hypocrites and bigots of "political correctness"'; p. 25). The final section, 'Interculturalism All the Same ...', seems designed to synthesise but in fact works hard to contain any disruption of the European perspective – and of course in its title and throughout represents 'us' as fundamentally 'all the same'. It consists of four essays by or about Barba and Grotowski and an optimistic concluding essay by Clive Barker celebrating 'The

Possibilities and Politics of Intercultural Penetration [*sic*] and Exchange'.

What this entrenchment of the west and the rest binary (from which the west inevitably benefits) derives from, I suggest, are attempts by Pavis to theorise intercultural performance within what is essentially a semiotics of communications, focusing on meaning production almost exclusively and enshrining a binary encoding–decoding model from communications theory. It also derives from attempts by Schechner, Victor Turner, and others to adopt an early anthropological model in which an objective, scientific 'us' studies and deploys an objectified, static 'them'. Indeed, in *Theatre at the Crossroads of Culture*, Pavis follows anthropologist Clifford Geertz in defining culture itself as 'a signifying system' (p. 8) and as a result concludes that 'intercultural communication is often possible only at the price of changing the mode of readability from one culture to another. The history of a text or a culture is nothing other than the history of the successive ways in which it has been read' (p. 205).

The exception to the semiotic modelling of interculturalism among the major texts of the 1990s is Bonnie Marranca and Gautam Dasgupta's valuable 1991 collection of essays from *Performing Arts Journal*, *Interculturalism and Performance*, where section and essay titles refer productively to '*Travels* in Culture', '*Currents* of Theatrical Exchange', and 'Kinds of *History*' (emphasis added), and where the editors offer non-semiotic definitions of interculturalism as 'a state of mind, as much as a way of working' (p. 11), and as 'a form of intertextualism' that can be understood to be dialogic

(p. 19). And the volume offers some potential routes out of the morass. Marranca herself notes the need to historicise and cosmopolitanise the intercultural (pp. 20–1), and contributor Mead Hunter, in an essay on 'Interculturalism and American Music', pleads for a '*responsible* way of employing this dangerous but promising outgrowth of postmodernity' (p. 295, emphasis added), a plea that turns away from mere aesthetic or formal analysis and interpretation towards the question of ethical and political use value.

Another issue with much 1990s work on the intercultural in performance is the increasingly problematic assumption of monocultural audiences as target cultures. As Fischer-Lichte observes in her essay 'Interculturalism in Contemporary Theatre', most of the twentieth-century interculturalists — among whom she includes American Robert Wilson working in Germany, Japan's Tadashi Suzuki, and Nigeria's Wole Soyinka, as well as Brook and others — 'direct their work primarily at the audience of their own culture' (p. 38). As we will see below, the increasingly mixed cultural make-up of urban centres around the world shakes the foundation of such assumptions and locates interculturalism no longer simply on the stage or between the stage and the auditorium but within the audience itself.

Finally, of course, there is the question of intent: what is the purpose of intercultural theatre and its analysis? For Fischer-Lichte, in 'Staging the Foreign as Cultural Transformation' (the essay that concludes *The Dramatic Touch of Difference*), it is clearly the same as it was for the modernists: the renewal of what she calls 'the own', or target culture, theatre (p. 279). For Pavis it is, somewhat surprisingly, the renewal less of the theatre than of the semiotic method of performance analysis. In *Theatre at the Crossroads of Culture* he argues:

> What is at stake [...] is the possibility of a universal, precise performance analysis and of an adequate notation system. [...] Instead of looking for further refinement of western performance analysis, we can institute another approach, the study of inter-cultural theatre, in the hope that it will produce a new way of understanding theatre practice and will thus contribute to promoting a new method-ology of performance analysis. (pp. 3–4)

But what if the purposes were different? What if the goals of intercultural exchange were less formal and aesthetic and more political, the methods less idealist and more material-ist, the understanding of audiences less monolithic, and the objects of analysis more multiplicitous? Perhaps under these circumstances the work of intercultural performance might more effectively function to redress rather than perpetuate the colonial project and might help to perform into being a more equitable basis for exchange.

Decolonising the stage

Perhaps not surprisingly, many from both sides of the inter-culture wars in the 1990s – including Bharucha, Chaudhuri, Chin, and Pavis himself – considered the theory and practice of interculturalism of the western, 'integrative' kind to have come to something of a stalemate almost as soon as it had been named. But there were rumblings from below all along and calls for a different kind of intercultural performance and research, the goals of which, in Schechner's terms, are 'disruptive'. There have also been, all along, intercultural performances designed to displace audiences rather than affirm their geocultural positionings, to take into account differences within as well as between national cultures, and to '*produce* the *experience* of difference', as Una Chaudhuri says in 'The Future of the Hyphen' (1991, p. 196, her emphasis). This type of intercultural practice, according to Andrzej Wirth in his contribution to Marranca and Dasgupta's *Interculturalism and Performance*, would subvert 'the conventional view that the theatre generated in a given country is an expression of its culture' (1991, p. 282). 'The flow of exchanges and transformations in the realm of Euro-American cultures [and, I would argue, elsewhere] asks for another model in which the very notion of source and target is invalidated' (p. 284).

Several works have addressed these calls for a new model of intercultural performance, chief among them the second, 'intracultural', half of Rustom Bharucha's 1993 book *Theatre and the World* and its 2000 sequel, *The Politics of Cultural Practice*; Christopher Balme's 1999 book *Decolonizing the Stage*, from which I take the title of this section (evoking, as Balme does, Ngugi wa Thiong'o's essential 1986 *Decolonising the Mind*, where the question of the language of address, albeit in fiction, is most powerfully taken up); Julie Holledge and Joanne Tompkins's 2000 book *Women's Intercultural Performance*; and Jacqueline Lo and Helen Gilbert's 2002 article in Schechner's journal, *TDR*, 'Toward a Topography of Cross-Cultural Theatre Praxis'. Each of these works valuably participates in the postcolonialist project of beginning to redress the historical genocides and continuing inequities of European imperialism, each complicates the east–west binary, and each makes a shift from aesthetic to political principles of intervention – or, more properly, insists that a narrow focus on the aesthetic is always already political insofar as it works to reify the currently dominant.

Bharucha is best known for his critiques of the western intercultural establishment, particularly the work of Brook, and many western academics have taken less note of his contributions to the theory and practice of what he calls *intra*culturalism within his native India. Bharucha uses 'intracultural' to refer to encounters between cultures within the nation-state rather than between nations, destabilising the problematic identification of (mono)culture with nation. He prefers intracultural over multicultural, as he explains in *The Politics of Cultural Practice*, because 'while the "intra" prioritizes the interactivity and translation of diverse cultures, the "multi" upholds a notion of cohesiveness' that polarises cultures and reifies cultural difference as static and unchanging (p. 9).

In the second and third sections of *Theatre and the World*, Bharucha describes and analyses intracultural projects within India that set out to rescue interculturalism from the stalemates of neo-colonialism, address or redress power imbalances in intercultural exchange, and incorporate 'detailed analysis of the social processes determining every-day life in other cultures' (p. 5). His account of his own involvement in the staging in India of German playwright Franz Xaver Kroetz's one-woman play *The Request Concert*, which features an Indian woman living within Indian social relations and material realities, genuinely attempts to con-sider the difficult question of equal exchange between cultures accorded differently valued roles within global the-atrical and political hierarchies. It also takes into account gender as well as race, class, and position within the theatre as institution – an Indian actress, for example, in relation to a male European text and male co-directors. Part three of *Theatre and the World*, and much of *The Politics of Cultural Practice*, worry away productively at the relationships within India between state support for traditional Indian perform-ance forms as (dormant, static) national 'heritage', the deployment of tradition within a nationalist agenda (perhaps functioning in complicity with western interculturalist valid-ations of 'authenticity'), and 'culturalist' assumptions about difference that efface material inequities. Bharucha also, crucially, introduces cross-cultural collaborations *between* 'othered' cultures that set aside the dominant western gaze and explore solidarities among marginalised cultures. In *The Theatre and the World*, for example, he brilliantly treats an adaptation of Nigerian novelist Chinua Achebe's clas-sic 1958 novel *Things Fall Apart* (its title already intercul-tural, evoking T. S. Eliot) by a cultural organisation called Ninasam in a small village in Karnataka in southern India, in collaboration with the transplanted Sidhu tribe, itself of African origin. In *The Politics of Cultural Practice* Bharucha usefully extends the range of his intracultural analysis to include under the rubric of culture such things as sexuality and the topics of religion and secularism, frequently avoided in the western academy as virtually taboo. But Bharucha's major contribution concerns the importance of the local and the material/real (the epigraph to *The Politics of Cultural Practice* is Walter Benjamin citing Brecht). His is a return, from the perspective of India, to the fundamental question of what intercultural or intracultural performance contributes to the lives and material realities of its local sources and audiences. As he says early in *Theatre and the World*, with literal biographical application to his own return to India from the American academy, 'my interculturalism has brought me home' (p. 9).

Christopher Balme comes from a very different place from Bharucha, both literally and in terms of his scholarly positioning. But like Bharucha, and explicitly, he is concerned with decolonising the stage. Balme is a *pā hekā* (white, settler) New Zealander who relocated to Germany. His 1999 book *Decolonizing the Stage: Theatrical Syncretism and Post-Colonial Drama* announces its project and (postcolonialist) approach in its title, along with its central argument about intercultural syncretism (merging). Balme's goal is to contribute to the understanding of the theatrical or performative response to imperialism, colonisation, and decolonisation; his archive is a wide range of Indigenous performances around the colonised world functioning within the framework of the western notion of theatre; and his approach is semiotic (concerned with the production of meaning), focusing on 'the process whereby culturally heterogeneous signs and codes are merged together', which he calls 'theatrical syncretism' (p. 1). The concept of syncretism is derived from comparative religion, particularly during the colonial period, and it signifies the process by which elements of two or more religions are merged to produce change. It is related to concepts such as créolisation or hybridity as used by postcolonial theorists, including Homi Bhabha in *The Location of Culture*, where he argues that 'the interstitial passage between fixed identifications opens up the possibility of a cultural hybridity that entertains difference without an assumed or imposed hierarchy' (p. 4). But 'syncretism' as Balme uses it gestures more directly to the creation of new theatrical *forms*.

Balme is concerned with meaning, and his focus is textual, but his version of semiotics is different from that of Pavis, in that it focuses on 'cultural texts' as carriers of meaning that are fully comprehensible only within the culture that produces and uses them. Most importantly, he is concerned with what happens when, in the hands of Indigenous or colonised artists, Indigenous performance elements are syncretised with the western theatrical tradition as a response to the western tendency to homogenise, to exclude, and to privilege formal, stylistic, racial, or cultural 'purity' (p. 8). He examines work written primarily in English from former colonies in Africa, the Caribbean, and India, as well as work by the Indigenous peoples of settler/invader cultures in New Zealand, Australia, and North

America, identifying three different types of Indigenous intercultural theatre:

1. forms that emerged when the western system of theatre was introduced to a culture that had no equivalent form or when existing forms were eclipsed but left traces of Indigenous performance elements in a thereby altered dominant form. Examples include the Yoruba travelling theatre in Nigeria and the commercial, British-style theatre that emerged in India during the nineteenth century

2. forms that are the result of an existing performance tradition adopting some features of western theatre but remaining structurally intact, as in Peking opera, Indian *kathakali*, or classical Japanese dance-theatre

3. essentially new forms that emerged from the more or less equal fusion of traditional forms with the formal properties of western dramaturgy, retaining the cultural integrity of both

Focusing in successive chapters on ritual frames, issues of language use, orality, the use of bodies, masks, dance, and music, and the experimental use of space, Balme addresses the ways in which Indigenous cultural texts are incorporated into and often alter western dramaturgical conventions, ultimately throwing into question some of the fundamental principles of western theatrical aesthetics – decolonising the stage. Among his dozens of examples is Nigerian playwright Wole Soyinka's use of Yoruban ritual forms, in which time

is suspended, to disrupt and question Aristotelian dramaturgical laws of temporal causality.

Because Balme concentrates on work produced by
Indigenous peoples within their own cultural context in
response to colonisation rather than on intercultural work
produced for western audiences under the synthesising control of western directors or playwrights, his book invaluably
complicates the linearity of Pavis's analysis. Its emphasis on
language, ritual, orality, and embodiment and the evocation
of Ngugi in his title also complicate western textuality and
raise crucial questions not only about the hierarchies of ver-
bal language in intercultural practice but also about the language of the body, issues of translation, and the negotiation
of meaning in performance. In his conclusion, however,
Balme acknowledges the fundamentally aesthetic nature of
much of his inquiry, which, moreover, avoids until its final
pages the question of the portability of the syncretic theatre
he examines and the ways in which local conditions of reception frame the possibilities for cross-cultural exchange.

Holledge and Tompkins's book *Women's Intercultural
Performance* shares with Balme's a postcolonial perspective
and a decision to feature intercultural work produced by
non-dominant groups. Unlike Balme, however, Holledge
and Tompkins concern themselves with the work of women,
their more materialist approach focuses less on aesthetics
than politics, and their method – locating 'culture' in 'the
construction of the self (or the subject position) and in the
context for that self' (p. 4) – is closer to cultural and performance studies than to semiotic analysis. Holledge and

Tompkins treat the site(s) of performance – whether considered to be the (female) bodies, the theatrical spaces, the postcolonial nations, or the transnational marketplaces in which it takes place – as sites of negotiation of the meanings that constitute both culture and human, female subjectivity. Drawing on feminist theory and women's experience in resisting the objectifications enacted on women and 'othered' cultures, they focus on the potential for a specifically *women's* intercultural performance to enact 'an exploration of intersubjectivity [...] not only through audience perceptions, but also through the motivations and subjective experience of artists', usefully seeing 'the space between intention and reception [as] a rich seam of intercultural enquiry' (p. 14).

Women's Intercultural Performance examines what happens to plot as Holledge and Tompkins trace the cultural exchange of Ibsen's *A Doll's House* and Sophocles' *Antigone* through Japan and China, Iran, and Argentina. They explore the divergent meanings attributed to Korean and Aboriginal women's ritual performances when they are staged in urban Australia. They address different cultural positionings of public and private space in 'returning home' plays from Algeria, South Africa, and Ghana, considering how geopolitical displacements produce multiple subject positionings in performance. They analyse the female performing body as the site of intercultural encounter, looking at Japanese women's performance in Australia and at solo performers from Japan and Québec who combine diverse cultural influences in their work. Here they usefully define three 'genres' of women's performance (pp. 112–50): the taxonomic (seeking to define the boundaries between cultures), the hybrid (seeking to merge cultures), and the nomadic (transgressing the boundaries of cultural and individual identity). Finally, in their most powerful and most materialist chapter, they consider the (largely devastating) impact of the international arts marketplace on the voluntary and involuntary traffic in women's performing bodies.

The central contributions Holledge and Tompkins make to the discourses of intercultural performance and the project of decolonising the stage are to foreground gender at length (astonishingly, for the first time) and to focus attention on the struggles women performers encounter in order to establish identity spaces and make larger cultural and political statements. This involves threading through their case studies a concern with the political, with the creation of new intercultural subjectivities, with the corporeal reality of the performing female body, and with the commodification of women and others in light of the globalisation of cultures. They conclude that '[u]ltimately the future of intercultural work is more likely to be tied to patterns of consumption than to idealistic notions of cultural exchange' (p. 182), but they call for more work on such things as intercultural performance time, dramaturgical structures, emotional expression, and audience–stage relations, invoking a second wave of women's intercultural performance that might manage to negotiate the vagaries of the marketplace in 'the indeterminant, transitional spaces that lie in between cultural certainties' (p. 183).

The first among the postcolonialists to attempt to offer an alternative schematic to Pavis's hourglass model of cultural exchange were Jacqueline Lo and Helen Gilbert, whose article 'Toward a Topography of Cross-Cultural Theatre Praxis' returns to Pavis in its use of 'cross-cultural' as an overarching category, under which Lo and Gilbert locate as subcategories the multicultural, postcolonial, and intercultural. Lo and Gilbert's purpose is less to survey the practices that together constitute cross-cultural theatre than to schematise (their essay is surprisingly taxonomic) and advance attempts to conceptualise those practices, and to explore 'the possibilities for cross-cultural theatre to radicalize and intervene in hegemonic arts practices' (p. 32). Somewhat unfairly, given the broad canvas of Holledge and Tompkins's attention to globalisation, they critique *Woman's Intercultural Performance*'s 'reluctance to engage with the "big picture"' as a failure 'to relate ethical issues to larger issues of knowledge formation within institutional, national, and global contexts' (p. 37) – a project that their own essay undertakes.

Lo and Gilbert divide the field of intercultural practice into three categories: the transcultural (what I have called the universalist), the intracultural (following Bharucha), and the extracultural (referring to 'theatre exchanges conducted along a West–East and North–South axis', p. 38). They consider 'modes of conducting intercultural theatre' along a continuum from the 'collaborative' (complex, community generated, and emphasising the process and politics of exchange) to the 'imperialistic' (product oriented and produced for the dominant culture's consumption), focusing on these operations primarily within the 'extracultural' category in the second half of their essay. Within this exploration are their best-known contributions: their critique of Pavis's hourglass model and their proposal of an alternative to it. The critique is based on two things: Pavis's central image of distillation, in which elements of the source (or 'other') culture are made manageable to the target culture by a process of boiling down, a reduction to essences that can easily be absorbed (p. 43); and his privileging of aesthetics over politics. Lo and Gilbert's new model functions as a kind of horizontal hourglass, created by bringing the thorny post-colonialist issues of agency, hybridity, and authenticity to bear on the anthropological and semiotic realms of intercultural performance. Ultimately, if not explicitly, their focus is on the most crucial (materialist) question that can be posed about intercultural performance: Who benefits?

The Lo and Gilbert model represents intercultural exchange as a two-way flow (like that of Pavis, the model does not schematise an exchange among more that two sources), with both partners considered as 'sources', while a target culture – the audience – is positioned along a continuum between them into which both feed. The strength of the model, Lo and Gilbert argue, is that it 'locates all intercultural activity within an identifiable socio-political context', but it does not, in fact, do so for its audience, the 'anticipated' but problematically uncharacterised 'target culture' (p. 45).

Lo and Gilbert conclude their essay with several productive discussions of 'organic' and 'intentional' hybridity, both of which might feature in any given production. The former involves the typically aesthetic fusion of cultural forms such as those Balme discusses; the latter involves the usually political process of negotiation and contestation. From this they proceed to a critique of essentialising notions of cultural authenticity, in which non-western cultural forms are assessed by standards of cultural purity that both fetishise them and relegate them to prehistoric or ahistorical realms of 'tradition'. Finally, they offer a brief analysis of sites of linguistic, situational, and embodied intervention into the discourses and practices of intercultural performance, asking such questions as: Whose language is used during the rehearsal process? Where does the project take place? How is power inscribed on and negotiated through the body? and How do those bodies encode difference? They end with a problem and a project. The problem they pose is 'how to avoid essentialist constructions of race and gender while still accounting for the irreducible specificity of certain bodies and body behaviours'. The project is to 'explore the rhizomatic potential of interculturalism – its ability to make multiple connections and disconnections between cultural spaces – and to create representations that are unbounded and open, and potentially resistant to imperialist forms of closure' (p. 47). We will return to these.

Critical intersections

It is clear that the relatively belated intersection of post-colonial theory with intercultural theatre studies produced a shift in perspective and politics from an overwhelming emphasis on the idealist and universalist to a more grounded focus on the localist and the historical, particularly as situated within former colonies. But what would it mean to consider the practice and study of intercultural performance in the light of homologous fields of scholarly inquiry that have come to prominence since the controversies over *The Mahabharata*, *L'Indiade*, and the other contested critical and performance texts at the heart of the interculture wars? What would it mean to apply the more recent insights of a newly configured performance studies, of critical multiculturalism, critical race theory and whiteness studies, diaspora studies, and new cosmopolitanism to the field of intercultural performance?

Performance studies

It may seem odd to include performance studies among the interdisciplines that have come recently to prominence, because, of course, performance studies and the study of intercultural theatre may be said to have the same parents – they may even be twins, however much they've grown apart. In her introduction to *The Ends of Performance*, which she co-edited with Jill Lane, Peggy Phelan refers to Richard Schechner and Victor Turner as the two men who 'gave birth' to performance studies (1998, p. 3), and the same might be said of the study of intercultural performance. The two fields emerged together during the late 1970s and early 1980s in Schechner's and Turner's anthropological/ethnographic approach to the study of ritual performance in non-western cultures and of performance in everyday life. In his theatrical practice, Schechner employed decontextualised versions of non-western ritual in productions such as his *Dionysus in 69* (The Performance Garage, New York, 1968), which incorporated a West Irian birth ritual into an adaptation of Euripides. Meanwhile, Turner somewhat absurdly experimented with having his students perform embodied versions of the 'cannibal' Hamatsa dance from the sacred winter ceremonials of the Kwakiutl people of Vancouver Island. According to Schechner, in his *Performance Studies: An Introduction*, performance studies emerged in part out of a desire for non-hierarchical intercultural multiplicity and (unproblematised) 'sympathy' for the marginalised, people of colour, and the formerly colonised, among others. However appropriative Schechner's and Turner's own practices may have been, these things clearly are potentially enabling for the development of intercultural performance forms that might move beyond the appropriative. Also enabling, and foundational to performance studies as a discipline, is the desire to shake up taxonomies, hierarchies, and disciplinary ownerships of what counts as a worthy object of study and the belief that *anything* can be studied as performance: a political demonstration, a religious ritual, a text, a painting, a street, a city – all can be analysed in terms of how they 'perform' in relation to whoever or whatever encounters them.

Performance studies, then, is omnivorous and open-ended, but some of its aspects and recent articulations have shifted the ground in ways that are particularly productive for the study of theatrical interculturalism. One, as articulated by the late Dwight Conquergood in his 2002 essay 'Performance Studies: Interventions and Radical Research', is the tendency for the field's combination of theory and practice to undermine 'textualism', to challenge the hegemony of the text in the academy, to resist the semiotic impulse to 'translate' world into text in order to make it an appropriate object of study, and to break down the borders between texts and bodies. Another is the 'performative turn' that allows us to understand gender, race, ethnicity, and other social identifiers not as biological or ontological but as *performative*, something one *does* rather than *has*, and thereby *performs into being*. Judith Butler, building on Schechner's definition of performance as 'restored', or 'twice-behaved', behaviour (detaching the behaviour from the person who performs it) and on the linguistic theories of J. L. Austin and John R. Searle, argued that gender, for example, 'is real only to the extent that it is performed' ('Performative Acts and Gender Constitution', 1988, p. 527). It is brought into being through rehearsal and ritual repetition. It is an act, albeit one that, as she says, 'has been going on before one arrived on the scene' (p. 526). If, as many have argued, this is true of social identifiers other than gender – identifiers such as race and ethnicity – then intercultural performance has the potential performatively to bring into being not merely new aesthetic forms but new social formations, new diasporic, hybrid, and intercultural social identities.

Critical multiculturalism studies

The theory and practice of intercultural theatre also have many parallels with the theory and practice of multiculturalism. Both begin, at least in theory, with humanist assumptions about the universal human condition and idealist visions of 'the brotherhood of man [*sic*]'. And both have been criticised for the violence these visions and assumptions can enact in practice in effacing real, material and cultural difference. In Australia and Canada, where official multiculturalism

policies have been adopted, critiques of state multiculturalism have focused on state attempts to manage (police or control) diversity in the wake of immigration policies dictated by
a historically specific need for cheap labour. Multiculturalist
policies and practices that concentrate on the preservation of
the (static) heritage of the 'other' and on containment within
a dominant society have given rise to critiques of the ghetto-
isation of 'othered' cultures and of discourses of 'tolerance'
promoted by Charles Taylor in 'The Politics of Recognition'
(1994). Tolerance, after all, is predicated on there being an
active subject who tolerates an 'other' who is thereby positioned as the passive object of a benevolent gaze, with some
presumed deficiency requiring patience and understanding.
In the case of multicultural policy and practice, this involves
a white, liberal 'we' who generously tolerate an ethnic 'them'
rather than dissolving into a transformed and hybrid multicultural entity. Sneja Gunew argues, in *Haunted Nations*, that
state multiculturalism has been 'framed by a liberal pluralism where cultural differences are paraded as apolitical
[ahistorical and static] ethnic accessories' (2004, p. 17) and
where women are most often positioned without agency
as the stolid bearers of the – respected to a fault – 'ethnic'
tradition, which often includes misogynist practices that are
construed as untouchable. Writing from the standpoint of
antiracist feminist Marxism in her book *The Dark Side of the
Nation*, Himani Bannerji has scrutinised what she calls 'capitalist state inspired multiculturalisms' (2000, p. 1) for their
capacity to obscure 'a hidden class struggle being conducted
behind cultural-historical masks of "authentic" identities'. She

critiques official multiculturalism's capacity to function 'as an epistemology of occlusion which displaces the actual living subjects, their histories, cultures, and social relations, with ideological constructs of ethnicity' (p. 11). The Canadian policy, she argues, operates by attributing social and economic inequalities, together with racialised and gendered violence, to 'cultural differences' rather than systemic racism and sexism. Finally, Abdul JanMohamed and David Lloyd, in *The Nature and Context of Minority Discourse* (1991), have argued convincingly that official multiculturalisms around the world promote a neo-liberal pluralism in which ethnic or cultural difference is merely an exoticism, an indulgence that can be relished without in any significant way threatening or modifying the dominant-culture individual who is securely embedded within the protective body of dominant ideology.

Critical multiculturalism (or 'resistance multiculturalism') grew out of critical pedagogy, on the one hand, and cultural studies, on the other. One of the field's main readers, *Critical Multiculturalism: Uncommon Voices in a Common Struggle* (1995), edited by Barry Kanpol and Peter McLaren, appeared in the Bergin and Garvey series 'Critical Studies in Education and Culture' edited by the founder of critical pedagogy, Paulo Freire, and its leading guru, Henry Giroux. This pedagogical branch of the field is grounded in hope and in solidarity across difference, whereas the cultural studies side has tended more towards radical critique. What the two share, and usefully bring to the theory and practice of intercultural performance, is a scepticism about national multiculturalisms, an

47

acute awareness of the ways in which official policies and public sentiments shape the conditions of the production and reception of intercultural practice, and a nevertheless utopian vision that is based on antiracist praxis.

Critical race theory

The roots of critical race theory are American. It emerged from the US legal academy and a 1970s activist sense that the civil rights movement of the 1960s, for all its apparent success, hadn't really changed things much. As a formal project, critical race theory crystallised in 1989 around a conference in a convent outside Madison, Wisconsin, building on critical legal studies and radical feminism to interrogate the role played by race in the American justice system. The approach was consolidated in 1995 in two massive anthologies of critical writing: Kimberlé Crenshaw, Neil Gotanda, Gary Peller, and Kendall Thomas's collection *Critical Race Theory: The Key Writings That Formed the Movement* and the first edition of Richard Delgado and Jean Stefancic's *Critical Race Theory: The Cutting Edge*, which was followed by a second edition in 2000. Critical race theory has since developed, multiplied, and spread to inhabit many fields, including theatre and performance studies, with the central project of historicising and deconstructing racial categorisation and critiquing the laws, customs, and systemic practices that authorise and enact it. Its major, foundational tenets are

- that racism is not aberrational but systemic (or 'ordinary')

- that racism serves the interests of a white dominant elite and working class who have little material interest in eradicating it
- that race does not, in scientific terms, exist but is invented, socially constructed, and historically variable – although the material consequences of its invention and application are very real
- that racialisation and racial characterisation are differential and variable, responding to historical shifts in labour and other markets as determined by the dominant culture
- that no person has her or his own unitary, essentialist identity; rather, everyone participates in identity construction that cuts across a range of categories including but not limited to race, ethnicity, gender, sexuality, class, and ability
- that minority status, particularly in solidarities across difference, authorises a privileged voice around issues relating to racialisation to which the dominant culture is unlikely to have direct access

Responses to racism have been analysed in critical race theory, in a familiar dichotomy, as being either idealist (responses that address and attempt to redress the ways in which race has been discursively constructed) or materialist (sometimes called realist; responses that consider the economic and social determinants that render racism systemic).

Critical race theory, as such, came late to theatre studies, as is evidenced by its inclusion as a category only in the second, 2007, edition of Janelle Reinelt and Joseph Roach's influential collection *Critical Theory and Performance*. Among the essays they include are the exemplary and distinctly intercultural essay by Jill Lane 'Black/face Publics: The Social Bodies of *Fraternidad*', in which Lane brings critical race feminism to bear on her analysis of the resistant performance of the multimedia *velada* in nineteenth-century Cuba, and Daphne Lei's 'Virtual Chinatown and New Racial Formation', which studies Cantonese opera in nineteenth-century San Francisco, as well as the (tourist) performance of Chinatown itself, 'the most Chinese place of all' (p. 156). What critical race theory brings to the theory and practice of intercultural performance is an acute, historicised awareness of race as constructed, or, more properly, performed; of racial and cultural identity and difference as fluid; of the intersectionality of social identities, where one can inhabit at once the social identities of a Black person, a woman, a lesbian, and a Jew; and of the problematic nature of black–white binary thinking (analogous to the west and the rest binary) that undermines potential solidarities across acknowledged difference.

Whiteness studies

An outgrowth or extension of critical race theory, whiteness studies reverses the ethnographic gaze, racialises whiteness, and investigates the invention of 'normal' (straight and white, as Julian B. Carter's 2007 book *The Heart of Whiteness* demonstrates, with its cover illustrations of an alabaster 1939 'Norma' and 'Norman'). The study of whiteness, particularly from the position of the 'other', is not new (one thinks of work such as Frantz Fanon's *Black Skin, White Masks*, which was published in English translation in 1967), but as a formal critical project it solidified in the early 1990s in books with titles such as *The Wages of Whiteness* (1991, by David R. Roediger), *Beyond the Pale* (1992, by Vron Ware), *The Invention of the White Race* (1994, by Theodore W. Allen), and *Towards the Abolition of Whiteness* (1994, by David R. Roediger). This activity culminated in 1997 with the appearance of Richard Dyer's groundbreaking book *White* – a study of representations of whiteness by white people, mainly in photography and film – along with three important readers: Richard Delgado and Jean Stefancic's monumental *Critical White Studies: Looking Behind the Mirror*, which they compiled as a sequel to their *Critical Race Studies* volume discussed above; Mike Hill's *Whiteness: A Critical Reader*, which focuses mainly on popular culture, mainly in the United States; and Ruth Frankenberg's *Displacing Whiteness*, in which whiteness is explored analytically as an international, multiracial, cross-class, and gendered phenomenon. The following year, cultural theorist George Lipsitz published his powerful, award-winning book *The Possessive Investment in Whiteness: How White People Profit from Identity Politics* (1998).

Whiteness studies begins by asking where whiteness comes from, how it became the ordinary, neutral fallback position from which 'others' could be viewed and judged, and how white became less a distinct race than the universal gold standard for the human race. It focuses on the relatively recent historical, legal, and cultural invention and maintenance of whiteness, on shifts and instabilities in whom one considers to be white (Jews, Italians, and the Irish in the United States having 'become' white relatively recently through economic advancement and class mobility), on the taken-for-granted universality of white privilege, and on the spectre of white supremacy. It documents, as Mike Hill argues, 'the struggle to remain "undistinguished" – the struggle to be ordinary, to be as passive as omnipresent, as invisible as dominant, to be an essential feature of everyday life *and yet unaccountable*' (p. 2, emphasis added).

Whiteness studies has made significant contributions to the discourses of intercultural theatre. Hill includes in his anthology an article by Kate Davy, 'Outing Whiteness', that focuses on feminist lesbian performance and one by Robert H. Vorlicky on 'Performing Men of Colour' that focuses on queer male autoperformance and 'the White Right'. Helen Gilbert, in a 2003 article in *Theatre Journal*, 'Black and White and Re(a)d All Over Again', draws on Dyer's concept of 'extreme whiteness' (in contrast to ordinary, unmarked whiteness) to provide a nuanced reading of the use of whiteface minstrelsy in plays by Murri playwright Wesley Enoch in Australia and Delaware Nation playwright Daniel David Moses in Canada. And in 2005 Mary F. Brewer published *Staging Whiteness*, which analyses twentieth-century British and American dramatic representations of whiteness. But in many ways the most significant contribution whiteness studies makes to the theory and practice of intercultural performance is to remind the white playwright, practitioner, or scholar that no whiteness can be taken for granted as neutral, invisible, unmarked, or 'unaccountable': it is a position from which to speak, work, and negotiate across acknowledged historical and material difference. As Dyer argues, 'the position of speaking as a white person is one that white people now almost never acknowledge and this is part of the condition and power of whiteness: white people claim and achieve authority for what they say by not admitting, indeed not realising, that for much of the time they speak only for whiteness' (p. xiv).

Diaspora studies

Whereas much of the focus of critical race and whiteness studies is intranational, often from an American perspective, diaspora studies begins with the historical and contemporary definitional fact of diaspora as the dispersion, dislocation, and migration of populations and cultures, usually involuntarily, from and across different geographical regions worldwide. Studies of the Jewish, African, and other diasporas go back centuries, but the consolidation of diaspora studies as a formal field is perhaps best dated to the founding of the journal *Diaspora* in 1991. Since then, the interdisciplinary field has attracted many of cultural theory's leading voices, including Arjun Appadurai, Rey Chow, Paul Gilroy, Stuart Hall, Evelyn Hu-DeHart, Lisa Lowe, Kobena Mercer, and Ella Shohat, among many others who have, for the most part, addressed diasporic formations within post-World War II nation-states. The sweep of the field has been broad and its reach global, and it has long since moved beyond understanding diasporic

communities as atomised, non-integrative, and engaged primarily in producing compensatory nostalgia for an idealised
homeland. Indeed, twenty-first-century diasporic communities, particularly in their second generations of immigration
and beyond, tend to be vibrant, adaptable, and predisposed to
intercultural solidarities. Diaspora studies is a complex and
productively contested field that now considers such issues as
the relationships between diaspora and nation; transnationalism and transmigration; tradition and modernity; localisation
and globalisation; territorialisation, deterritorialisation, and
reterritorialisation; ethnicisation and assimilation; exile and
return; diasporic traversals and identity formation in relation
to race, ethnicity, gender, and sexuality; 'ethnic absolutism'
(in Paul Gilroy's phrase in his foundational 1993 book *The
Black Atlantic*); and the lived experience of multiply diasporic
peoples scattered across the globe and concentrated within
specific areas. Centrally, the very existence of diaspora
enforces a rethinking of nation, nationalism, and citizenship,
on the one hand, and, on the other, offers multiple and complex sites for contesting, on a transnational scale, the homog-
enising forms of late capitalist McGlobalisation.

For the study of intercultural performance, diaspora
studies most promisingly offers a model for analysing the
performative intercultural constitution of diasporic identities beyond the 'home' nation; ways of understanding the
reappropriation and refiguring in diaspora of the performance forms of 'home' cultures (a process that resembles
what Joseph Roach, in his 1996 book *Cities of the Dead*, calls
'surrogation'); and a model, in conjunction with critical

multiculturalism studies, for the analysis of the intersection of a variety of cultures within urban multicultural settings in the new 'global city' – an issue to which we will return.

Intercultural performance studies have contributed significantly to diaspora studies, in part because diasporic identities are so clearly performative. Among the best examples of this contribution is a special issue of the journal *Modern Drama*, guest edited in 2005 by Yan Haiping and titled *Other Transnationals: Asian Diaspora in Performance*. The issue is noteworthy for its focus on the lived experiences of Asian diasporic performers globally; its refusal to locate the United States, the North, or other western cultures at the centre of diaspora studies or as the assumed destination for all sojourners; and its refusal to solidify a western-centric version of 'Asia' (which, as Yan points out, is a British invention). The special issue includes essays about an opera performer from a small socialist village in northeast China dislocated to dubious success in the global city of Hong Kong and irretrievably alienated from her small-town home and family; Filipino bands performing American hit songs in five-star hotels across Asia to support their families, with whom they interact almost exclusively through the Internet; South Africans of 'Indian origins'; an Iranian performer playing out her diasporic identities in the United States; and a Korean-Japanese-American, cast by Hollywood as a 'generic Asian', who returns home. Yan provides an introduction that productively critiques celebratory, neo-idealist visions of 'the diasporic subject' (usually a new, elite class of multiple passport holders complicit in the operations of mobile global capital). But she also provides a compelling account of efforts to counter the totalising effects of globalisation by defining and accounting for a 'living world with radically changing human configurations and deeply conditioned, but intensely active struggles for possible agency' (p. 230). She finds, indeed, in 'the bodily rhythms of the diasporic [subject] not only signs of strivings for resettlement but also desires for survival in transit that are potentially or effectively transformative' (p. 237). Finally, she discovers, in performed 'trans-nation' and in the *choice* (as opposed to the 'ethnic destiny') of becoming diasporic, 'a material space of alternative temporality, where new alliances and forms of citizenry as flexible social solidarity become tangible' (p. 241). This newly discovered diasporic transnational network, Yan argues, can potentially contradict and undermine the structural ambitions of global capital (p. 241).

Critical cosmopolitanisms

Cosmopolitanism has a long and inglorious post-Enlightenment lineage and linkage to colonialist knowledge systems that produced and continue to reify the gap between the west and the rest as the subjects and objects of 'human' knowledge production. After all, Immanuel Kant's 'universal cosmopolitan existence', as articulated in his 1784 essay 'The Idea of Universal History from the Cosmopolitan Point of View' (included in his *Political Writings*, 1990, p. 51), essentially excluded Black and Native peoples from 'proper personhood'. But there is a new critical cosmopolitanism – or rather there are several — that attempts to circumvent the traps of universalism and multiculturalism. Helen Gilbert and Jacqueline Lo, in *Performance and Cosmopolitics*, list James Clifford's 'discrepant cosmopolitanism', Mitchell Cohen's 'rooted cosmopolitanism', Benita Parry's 'postcolonial cosmopolitanism', and Pnina Werbner's 'working-class cosmopolitanism' as 'middle-path alternatives between ethnocentric nationalism and particularistic multiculturalism' with the general aim of remaking cosmopolitanism into 'a more worldly and less elitist concept' — a kind of cosmopolitanism-from-below (pp. 4—5) that is perhaps more palatable for many than the pieties of state multiculturalism. As Australian journalist Hugh Mackey observes, 'cosmopolitanism sounds like something we achieved, not something that was imposed on us' (qtd. p. 17).

Performance and Cosmopolitics is itself the best illustration of the value of the new cosmopolitanisms for the study of intercultural theatre. Gilbert and Lo divide the new cosmopolitanisms into three categories (pp. 4—10): (1) neo-Kantian 'moral/ethical' cosmopolitanisms that particularise and pluralise Kant's abstract category of the human in what Kwame Anthony Appiah, in 'Cosmopolitan Reading' (2001), calls 'universalism plus difference'; (2) 'political' cosmopolitanism, which involves efforts to establish transnational legal and political frameworks that can deal with the consequences of economic globalisation and move towards a 'cosmopolitan democracy' that recognises the principle of multiple loyalties to different communities; and (3) 'cultural' cosmopolitanisms, which consist of an attitudinal openness to cultural difference combined with a practice of navigating across cultural boundaries. Arguing that cosmopolitanism 'is increasingly gaining purchase as a form of sociocultural capital' (p. 10) and pointing out 'the ways in which specific ideological positions unravel at the point of embodiment' – that is, performance (p. 12) – they set out to examine how, in practice rather than theory, the sociocultural capital of these new cosmopolitanisms circulates in a wide range of Australian performance practices, both intranationally and internationally. Their central contribution is to argue that 'there is, inevitably, a politics to the practice of cosmopolitanism – a *cosmopolitics* that is caught up in hybrid spaces, entangled histories, and complex human corporeographies [geographies of the body]' (p. 11, emphasis in original). They celebrate many of the successes of evolving Aboriginal, Asian, and cross-cultural performance cultures, particularly effectively for our interculturalist purposes looking at 'Aborasian' alliances that bypass white brokerage. But they are most effective because they carefully locate their analysis within specific national and global social, cultural, and political contexts and because of their nuanced scrutiny of complex negotiations across different stakes and scripts, as the dangers involved in risking assimilation, co-optation, codification (labelling), and exoticisation trade off against the potentialities of new visibility, awareness, and mutual accommodation.

Intercultural performance ecologies

Taken together, what these relatively new critical approaches I have been surveying bring to the theory and practice of intercultural theatre are tools for the analysis of a new kind of rhizomatic (multiple, non-hierarchical, horizontal) intercultural performance-from-below that is emerging globally, that no longer retains a west and the rest binary, that is no longer dominated by charismatic white men or performed before audiences assumed to be monochromatic, that no longer involves the urban centres (in the west or elsewhere) raiding traditional forms seen to be preserved in more primitive or 'authentic' rural settings, and that no longer focuses on the individual performances or projects of a single artist or group. The new interculturalism, as I see it, involves collaborations and solidarities across real and respected material differences within local, urban, national, and global intercultural performance ecologies. I use the word 'ecology' in relation to embodied, theatrical, urban, national, transnational, or virtual intercultural spaces for two reasons: first, everything that happens within an eco-system affects everything else within that system; second, the health of an ecosystem is best judged by the diversity of its species rather than by the competitive success of indi-vidual components or species. These performance ecologies function as heterotopias – 'spaces of alternate ordering', in Kevin Hetherington's definition in *The Badlands of Modernity* (1997, p. viii) – and they serve to forge what Holledge and Tompkins, in *Women's Intercultural Performance*, call 'new identity spaces' (p. 178). These do not function merely as sites of semiotic intersection, or as postmodern collages, but as politicised sites for the constitution of new, hybrid, and diasporic identities in space.

What is happening now in increasingly multicultural urban centres globally is the development of performance ecologies in which Indigenous and immigrant minoritised populations are working performatively to forge diasporic identities in relation not to the dominant culture – or not to the dominant cultural alone – but to one another. Where performance forms that have emerged in the past have tended to be hybrid primarily under the sign of the hyphen (African-American, Indo-African, Chinese-Filipino, and so on) and to function in a binary, resistant relationship to the dominant, in the twenty-first century, cross-cultural intersections tend to be both horizontal (as in the 'Aborasian' work discussed by Gilbert and Lo) and more multiple (collaboratively engaging more communities). Consequently, they call for new theoretical approaches for their analysis. Hourglass models, vertical or horizontal, were perhaps adequate to trace the types of early and mid-twentieth-century borrowings, decontextualisations, and appropriations of 'othered' forms by decadent western theatrical cultures in need of renewal. And early postcolonial, oppositional models of resistance, together with counterhegemonic nationalisms, were at one point necessary to resist the most overt forms of colonial domination (though they tended to reinscribe binaries, reify the dominance of the dominant, and construct their own internal exclusions). But what is needed now, drawing on the complexities and insights of performance studies, critical multicultural studies, diaspora studies, new cosmopolitanisms, and so on, is a model of scholarly praxis that is humble before the dizzying multiplicities of its objects of study, that is cognisant of the researcher's own positioning and the process of scholarship as itself necessarily intercultural performance, and that does its homework in terms of attempting to understand cultural and performance forms in situ. Finally, what is needed is a model of scholarship that understands the multiple performances of difference, local and global, as *processes*, circulations of energy, in which previously marginalised cultures are seen to work *together* rather than *against*, constructing genuine, rhizomatic, and multiple intercultures that respect difference while building solidarities. And in practice, this is happening.

An example of the kind of intercultural performance ecology that I have in mind is coming into being in the city of Toronto, which calls itself 'the world's most multicultural city', though it has competition for this title from London, New York, and Sydney. Such competitions, of course, risk reifying western, settler/invader colonies as diasporic destinations and ignoring the kinds of intercultural flow Yan Haiping foregrounds in her expanded Asia. But Delhi, Dublin, Rio, Stuttgart, Amsterdam, Yokohama, and dozens of other cities are increasingly sites of intercultural exchange, and groups such as director Amal Allana's New Delhi company, in staging an adaptation of Colombian novelist Gabriel García Márquez's *Eréndira* in 2004 that blended rhythms, movements, and costumes from India and Latin America, are increasingly common and provide food for thought. My focus on Toronto, however, comes in part because it is my 'local', in part because it serves as the intersection of hundreds of diasporas – its name is said to derive from the

Huron word for 'meeting place' between diverse pre-contact Indigenous cultures – and in part because its multicultural-ism today involves both immigrants and Indigenous peoples of the Americas, who come together in the city as a kind of 'Indian diaspora' (a term which is productively problematic in referring to a diasporic condition *within* the homeland).

In the past decade a vibrant, interdependent ecology of intercultural performance has emerged in Toronto, crossing cultures and performance disciplines and beginning to reflect the cultural differences that are visible and audible on the city's streets and in its streetcars. Some theatre companies, such as the Filipino Carlos Bulosan Theatre, are dedicated to supporting and reflecting specific cultural communities, and work on their productions can feel like the mutual teaching and rehearsing of how to be Filipino in diaspora – along with how to come together as a diasporic community across cul-tural differences internal to the Philippines and the Filipino diaspora. Others – companies such as the AfriCan Theatre Ensemble, Theatre Archipelago, and Rasik Arts – primarily perform work from cultural 'homelands', in these cases Africa, the Caribbean, and South Asia respectively, balancing cultural preservation, compensatory nostalgia, and the for-ging of new social subjectivities. Others still, such as Obsidian Theatre, b current, fu-GEN Asian-Canadian Theatre, Aluna and Alameda theatres, Red Sky Performance, and Native Earth Performing Arts *constitute* internally diverse cultural communities *as* 'African Canadian', 'Caribbean Canadian', 'Asian Canadian', 'Latino Canadian', 'Aboriginal', and 'Native Canadian', respectively, developing and performing new work that speaks across significant differences internal to these communities-in-diaspora. Finally, companies such as Cahoots Theatre Projects, Modern Times, and the feminist Nightwood Theatre (since the inauguration of their new mandate in 1989 dedicated to women of colour) are yet more broadly and explicitly *inter*cultural. Each of these companies mounts one or two productions per year, and many of them are also, and crucially, involved in developing, workshopping, and presenting new work at fringe and play development festivals such as SummerWorks, b current's rock.paper.sistahz festival, Factory Theatre's intercultural CrossCurrents festival, and the AfriCanadian Playwrights Festival, and this work is increasingly visible in the regular subscription seasons of mainstream companies before audiences who are themselves increasingly diverse.

In my essay 'Multicultural Text, Intercultural Performance' (2009) I discuss some of the ways in which these companies have employed such tactics as strategic reappropriation, diasporic transnationalism or transindigeneity, and urban interculturalism in their work.

Strategic reappropriation

The first tactic, involving the reappropriation of canonical work that has participated in the project of colonisation, is familiar from early postcolonial plays such as Aimé Césaire's *Une tempête* (Festival d'Hammamet, Tunisia, 1969) and has been documented in volumes such as Craig Dionne and Parmita Kapadia's *Native Shakespeares: Indigenous Appropriations on a Global Stage* (2008). Toronto examples include Djanet Sears's

63

well-known African Canadian response to *Othello*, *Harlem Duet*, which was first produced in 1997 by Toronto's feminist Nightwood Theatre at the Tarragon Extra Space. *Harlem Duet* tells the story of Othello's Black first wife, Billie, and in doing so reverses Shakespeare's representation of Othello as an isolated, tragic character in an overwhelmingly white world (and naturalised European culture). It relocates the play to Harlem, the centre of African North American diasporic culture. There it is Shakespeare who is isolated and decentred, surrounded on the bookshelves by volumes such as *African Mythology* and *Black Psychology*, and surrounded in the play by central moments, speeches, and images from Black history. Indeed, if on one level the play takes place at the intersection of Shakespeare and Black North American culture, it most literally takes place at the heart of that culture, at the intersection of Harlem's Martin Luther King and Malcolm X Boulevards. The play's 'duets' are played out between the assimilationist Othello ('at a deeper level we're all the same') and the separatist Billie ('I'm not the same'), representing the respective positions of those two great African American leaders (1997, p. 54). But the play also directly represents the history of slavery and blackface minstrelsy in its crucial 1860 and 1928 actions, which are played virtually as flashbacks – that is, deeply embedded and embodied cultural memories – by the same actors who play Billie and Othello in the present-tense action. The play evokes identity-forming cultural icons, painting an epic cultural canvas in its dialogue and between-scene interludes: the Harlem Renaissance and Langston Hughes, the Apollo Theatre, the Underground

Railroad, Marcus Garvey, Aretha Franklin, Sojourner Truth, Louis Farrakhan, Jesse Jackson, Christopher Darden (of the O. J. Simpson trial), Anita Hill (of the Clarence Thomas hearings), the Declaration of Independence, the Emancipation Proclamation, the LA riots, the Million Man March, Paul Robeson, Ira Aldridge, and the blues.

Native Earth Performing Arts has also reappropriated Shakespeare, in *Death of a Chief* (National Arts Centre, Ottawa, 2008), an adaptation of *Julius Caesar* by a collective of performers from various First Nations. But whereas Sears, in *Harlem Duet*, had at once claimed and finally rejected Shakespeare – 'the Shakespeare's mine, but you can have it', says Billie, dividing the bookshelves at the dissolution of her marriage (1997, p. 52) – the anticipated postcolonial critique in *Death of a Chief* was replaced by a project that generally accepted the cultural authority and 'universality' of Shakespeare but laid claim to that authority and that universality. The Native Earth production used Shakespeare for its own ends, analysing through Shakespeare the post-contact poison that has infected Native communities, particularly in relation to the fight for self-government, since the beginnings of the colonial project – even though that project was also *effected*, in part, through strategic deployments of Shakespeare as required reading in the colonies and evidence of European cultural superiority. One of the goals of the production was to provide essential training that is often denied to First Nations and Aboriginal actors; another was to deflect the pain of internal betrayals within the community, and the exposing of those betrayals in performance, onto Shakespeare's exposition of the dysfunctions at the root of European history. But chief among the goals of *Death of a Chief* was to perform into existence, through engagement with Shakespeare, an intercultural Native diasporic community in Toronto out of the many displaced First Nations that find themselves there. The development workshop through which the show was generated drew on Shakespeare's representation of early European history to explore crises in leadership within the Native community, using the negotiations involved in the workshop format to forge community identities across differences among contemporary First Nations cultures. The workshop began with a negotiation among the company members about the ceremonial elements of ritual performance in their various cultural traditions. As Native Earth's artistic director, Yvette Nolan, said in an unpublished interview with me in 2006:

> [W]hen you put people in a room together, you
> end up with a discussion of what those traditions
> are, and who they've learned them from, and
> that's what they bring into the room. It's inter-
> esting when we work on a project like *The Death
> of a Chief*, which has, at any given time, between
> eight and fifteen Aboriginal artists in the room.
> [...] All of those people bring all of their trad-
> itions to the room and then we have a negotiation,
> and we agree on the things that we can agree on,
> and it works just like it says in the stories that
> it works, in that we sit and discuss it until we
> figure out what everyone can live with.

Ultimately, 'we created our own ritual', Nolan says. It is important to notice here the ways in which Native Earth draws upon and respects traditional performance forms without engaging in the preservationist rhetoric of Canada's official multicultural policies. The newly created rituals are respectful but negotiated ones used to forge diasporic urban identities across First Nations. *Death of a Chief*, then, which began as a series of workshops with no firm plans for a production, was processual – heterotopic – in intent. The hope was, according to Nolan, that 'if we can work it out in this play then maybe we can work it out in our lives too'.

A third mode of intercultural reappropriation is represented by the work of Modern Times Stage Company, which has also presented reappropriations of Shakespeare (*Macbeth* at The Theatre Centre in 2005, *Hamlet* at Theatre Passe Muraille in 1999), along with classics from Persian culture, but whose mandate under artistic director Soheil Parsa is the blending of eastern with western forms and the creation of culturally inclusive alternative theatre experiences. This blending results in productions that are determinedly modernist but with a reappropriative twist, as in the case of *bloom*, written by Argentinian Canadian Guillermo Verdecchia and staged at The Theatre Centre in 2006, which featured stunning performances by Indian dancer and actor Anita Majumdar as 'the boy' and veteran 'white' Toronto actor Andrew Scorer as Gerontion. *bloom* began as an adaptation of T. S. Eliot's *The Waste Land*, but because of permission problems with the Eliot estate, the show was finally presented as having been 'inspired by' Eliot's modernist epic. Like most Modern Times productions, *bloom* is most interesting for its intercultural appropriations of modernism itself, its skirting of the modernist–capitalist alignment over ownership, and its representing-with-a-difference the high modernist appetite for the consumption of 'other' cultures. Ultimately, the play productively misrepresents Eliot's own work among the fragments that an unsettled 'we' shore against our ruins in the savage, post-apocalyptic world in which it is set.

Diasporic transnationalism and transindigeneity

In recent years, as Yasmeen Abu-Laban and Christina Gabriel have argued, official Canadian multiculturalism has moved increasingly towards *Selling Diversity*, as the title of their book has it: appropriating multiculturalism in the service of globalisation. But these authors also note the capacity for a kind of strategic transnationalism to perform globalisation differently, rehearsing modes of alternate ordering, pointing to 'groups and individuals who contest policy changes and new directions', 'actors [who] may themselves be part of new transnational networks and organizations that supercede national boundaries' (2002, p. 22).

The clearest and simplest theatrical expressions of this type of transnationalism have to do with maintaining connections with cultural 'homelands' and building diasporic networks. Thus theatre companies such as the AfriCan Theatre Ensemble, Theatre Archipelago, and Rasik Arts have been largely dedicated to producing plays from their respective homelands. Despite some residual tendency to promote compensatory nostalgias among first-generation immigrants, these companies have often introduced major works from the international repertoire to Toronto, contributing to the productive internationalisation of Canadian multiculturalism and introducing and keeping active performative forms of difference. They have also, of course, excited new diasporic awarenesses, in that the communities they performatively constitute cut across the boundaries of nation-states *within* their respective homelands.

First Nations companies such as Red Sky Performance and Turtle Gals Performance Ensemble – despite Aboriginal and First Nations peoples having been neglected by official Canadian multiculturalism (or perhaps because of that enabling neglect), despite their having little purchase in the realm of global capital, and despite working within very different diasporic contexts – have proven themselves expert at forging transnational, transindigenous connections. Since its founding in 2000 by artistic director Sandra Laronde, Red Sky has worked out of Toronto with Indigenous performers – writers, actors, musicians, and dancers – from Canada, the United States, Mexico, Australia, and Mongolia to bring the traditional forms of a worldwide diasporic Aboriginal community into the realm of the contemporary avant-garde. Red Sky eschews purely text-based work and avoids 'issue' plays, focusing on what, in an interview with me in 2006, Laronde called the 'beauty' of Aboriginal peoples and concerning itself with the contemporary celebration of transindigenous Aboriginal identities. But in drawing on traditional Aboriginal forms 'to articulate a contemporary dance process while creating new movement vocabularies', as Rebecca Todd has argued in her article 'Enlivening the Land' (2003, p. 24), Laronde sometimes skirts dangerously close to the familiar high modernist practice of renewing western high culture by incorporating, absorbing, and commodifying 'primitive' forms, even as her courting of new audiences through celebratory Aboriginal dance risks exoticism and collusion with problematic official multiculturalisms.

Rustom Bharucha's analysis of tradition and theatre in India, and in particular his case study of Shivaram Karanth's Yaksharanga (an adaptation of the traditional Karnataka music/dance form Yakshagana) in *Theatre and the World*, provides some useful insights here. Bharucha's concern is with what he calls (following Eric Hobsbawm) 'the invention of tradition', the making of new artefacts 'through the intervention and assimilation of "foreign" structures of representation' (p. 193). It is important to note that, in the case of Native theatre in Canada, these 'foreign' structures are colonialist in origin and include the forms and conventions of theatre itself, which necessarily mediate all staged Indigenous performance. Chief among these structures are the proscenium stage, the conventions of stage sound and lighting, and the power relations embodied in them all. The relatively unaltered traditional grass dance in Red Sky's *Shimmer* (Canada Dance Festival, National Arts Centre, Ottawa, 2006), performed in full regalia by Matthew Pheasant, a champion Anishinabe grass dancer from Manitoulin Island, and an unreconstructed pow-wow-style fancy dance by Oneida champion Nigel Schuyler, viewed through the representational technology of Toronto's Harbourfront Centre, might serve as examples

of reinventions of tradition that come from external intervention, in Bharucha's distinction, rather than from the
natural growth of traditional performance (p. 196). To this
non-Native viewer, both dances seemed exotic and decorative show stoppers, and the show as a whole was viewed and
reviewed as such outside of the Native community.

This is not to say that Red Sky is producing in *Shimmer*
either 'authentic' Aboriginal performance (with all the
colonialist preoccupations with purity and identity that
term implies) or a 'tourist show'. Like Shivaram Karanth
in Bharucha's account, they are producing 'a well-made
ballet that is tightly co-ordinated, accessible, and emi-
nently exportable' (p. 203). But the exportability of Red
Sky's work is similarly risky: what at home feels like the
celebration of a strong and vibrant contemporary Native
community in the face of ongoing external pressure can
feel very different on the touring circuit. As Red Sky tours
its celebratory shows internationally with the support of
an impressive list of private foundations and funds from all
levels of government – including, unusually for a theatre
company, the federal Department of Foreign Affairs and
International Trade – it risks serving the role of Canadian
cultural ambassador in ways with which many Native
people may not be comfortable. It is perhaps not accidental
that Sandra Laronde has received a degree of national recognition and support usually reserved for more senior artists.

Many in the Native community might wonder at what
cost this full citizenship in the Canadian nation comes.
Indeed, one wonders whether the showcasing of celebratory
Native performance as international diplomacy might serve

to mask, for example, ongoing concerns about Canada's
historical and contemporary treatment of its Native
peoples. But Laronde presses on, refusing to allow herself
to be discouraged by the type of negativity that she sees
as a debilitating leftover from colonialism. Typically, she
moves forward, creating work for and increasing the pro-
file of Aboriginal performers in Canada and abroad, insist-
ently rewriting dominant media images of Native peoples by
replacing racist stereotypes with representations of aston-
ishing beauty and skill, and tactically exploiting the pieties
of Canada's official multiculturalism to advance the cause
globally of Aboriginal people in the arts.

Native Earth has also negotiated the discourses of globalisation through collaborations with Indigenous peoples
rather than national governments, but theirs is a transindigeneity that largely circumvents the industrial model of production and diplomatic exchange through touring as 'foreign
relations' or globalised free trade in commodified cultures.
Rather than collaborations within a single production, Native
Earth's Honouring Theatre project involved a repertory system of mounting and touring productions by Aboriginal companies from Canada, Australia, and New Zealand to all three
countries in 2006–8, and the collaboration continues. It
involves forging strategic alliances that bypass white brokerage, 'establishing', as the tour's programme put it, 'indigenous trade routes through the arts' that echo pre-contact
trade routes among Indigenous nations, and 'creating global
pathways for indigenous theatre'. This ambitious project
initially staged and toured Nolan's own play *Annie Mae's
Movement* (Nakai Theatre, Whitehorse, Yukon, 1998),

Injibarndi/Palku playwright David Milroy's memory play *Windmill Baby* (Subiaco Theatre Centre, Perth, Western Australia, 2005), and Samoan playwright Makerita Urale's evocative text and movement piece *Frangipani Perfume* (BATS Theatre, South Auckland, New Zealand, 2005). The companies include actors and directors from a range of Indigenous Nations from North America and the South Pacific who came together over three countries and three years.

Like Red Sky, Turtle Gals Performance Ensemble, founded in Toronto in 2000 by Jani Lauzon, Monique Mojica, and Michelle St. John, was concerned, until it folded in 2008, with exploring a continuum of past, present, and future expressed as stories. The ensemble drew on traditional forms of storytelling, oratory, song, and dance and integrated them with current technology and popular culture to develop non-linear multidisciplinary theatre forms. And like Red Sky, their interest exceeded and exploded national boundaries to take in, in their case, the Indigenous peoples of the Americas.

The form of the Turtle Gals' work was hybrid; in fact, the work's formal hybridity reflected and grew out of the performers' own mixed race, which also served as the at-once hemispheric and autobiographical content of their work. This was autobiography in the broadest sense of the term: autobiography that spans the generations and reaches throughout the Americas. The name Turtle Gals referenced their sense of rootedness in the continental context of Turtle Island (North America), as did their inheritance of the mantle of New York's Spiderwoman Theater — the longest-running Native theatre company in North

America — through Mojica's training and family connections. Both Mojica and St. John were raised in the United States. The Kuna and the Rappahannock, from whom Mojica and the women of Spiderwoman (Mojica's mother and maternal aunts) descend, are the Indigenous people, respectively, of Kuna Yala, an autonomous territory on the coast of Panama, and of Virginia, on the East Coast of the United States. St. John's ancestry is Wampanoag, from what is now southeastern Massachusetts. Lauzon is of Métis (mixed western and Indigenous) ancestry in land that is now Canada. More generally, in her 2006 'rant' 'Of Borders, Identity, and Cultural Icons', Mojica has denied the relevance of the latter-day borders of nation-states to her own work and that of Turtle Gals, except as an encumbrance, and she has elsewhere in 2006, in an article entitled 'Stories from the Body', explicitly articulated a sense that the 'blood memory' of her own pan-American ancestry surfaces in that work. Indeed, her own 1990 play *Princess Pocahontas and the Blue Spots*, performed at the Back Space, Theatre Passe Muraille, with Indigenous Chilean musician Alejandra Nuñez, which models many of the processes and forms developed further in the work of Turtle Gals, functions as a kind of composite autobiography of mixed-race women (and the mothers of mixed-race peoples) across the Americas.

All of this — the autobiographical, the hybrid, the hemispheric, the traditional, and the contemporary, together with a deeply rooted sense of First Nations cultural memory — played itself out in Turtle Gals' complex and provocative interdisciplinary productions. *The Scrubbing Project* (Factory Studio Café, Toronto, 2002, 2006–7) was the company's signature piece and its most directly auto-biographical show, dealing with the writer/performers' own hybridised identities, their own internalised racism, and their own experiences 'living with genocide', as the play's darkly comic 'support group' is called ('my name is Blessed Ophelia and I am living with genocide'). But it also dealt, as Anishinabe scholar Jill Carter points out in her article 'Writing, Righting, "Riting"', with the 'recovery, remembrance, revitalisation and reintegration of *all* Aboriginal peoples' regardless of their current national location (2006, p. 14, emphasis in original).

Urban intraculturalism

Finally, theatre companies across Toronto's intercultural performance ecology have developed a kind of co-operative urban intraculturalism-from-below in order to perform differently the corporate drive within Canada's official multicultural policy towards 'internal globalisation' – multiculturalism deployed as market advantage for Canadian exports within the 'home' nations of its diasporic communities. These theatre companies might be thought of as adapting Bharucha's call for a grass-roots theatrical *intra*culturalism, constructing a heterotopic space within the city. The contemporary intercultural performance ecology of Toronto is a complex web of interconnections among individuals and companies working in solidarity across their acknowledged differences to challenge the hegemony of whiteness on the city's stages. Yvette Nolan calls this informal network 'the brown caucus', and in an unpublished interview with me in the summer of 2006 gives a sense of how it functions:

> The Native Earth office consists of two Aboriginal women, one Black woman, and one Asian woman, and we bring all our communities to the work. We always choose *other* in the work. So when we choose directors, designers, dramaturges, we all choose *other*. Even though Weesagechak [Begins to Dance] is an Aboriginal festival developing work by Aboriginal writers, we first choose *other* dramaturges, dramaturges who are Aboriginal or who are Asian or who are queer. *Other* as in not white, not from the dominant culture, those who in some way have a sense of self outside of or beside the dominant culture.

The urban geography of contemporary downtown Toronto facilitates working across difference. As urban planners Mohammed Qadeer and Sandeep Kumar found in a 2006 study, 'Ethnic Enclaves and Social Cohesion', the city's downtown is largely free of the concentrations of single eth-nic communities that they call ethnic enclaves, which are now more characteristic of the suburbs. Downtown neigh-bourhoods are mixed and flow into one another, allowing for the performance of genuinely intercultural exchange and genuine intercultural identities not pre-scripted by offi-cial multiculturalism.

Native Earth's offices are in Toronto's arts-centred Distillery District, next to the offices of Nightwood Theatre, one floor below those of Modern Times Stage

Company, and not far from the Carlton Street offices of
fu-GEN or the Queen Street East home bases of Obsidian
and Cahoots. One of Native Earth's office staff at the time
of my interview with Nolan, Nina Lee Aquino, was also
founding artistic director of fu-GEN, playwright in resi-
dence at Cahoots Theatre Projects, director of a recent
production at Carlos Bulosan, artistic producer of the
CrossCurrents intercultural play development festival at
Factory Theatre, where she had also been apprentice artistic director, and as of 1 September 2009 was the newly
appointed artistic director of Cahoots Theatre Projects.
And her resume is not unique. Second-generation Chinese
Canadian actor and playwright Keira Loughren has been
artistic producer, with African Canadian Kimahli Powell,
of SummerWorks, the city's vibrant and diverse new-play
festival. Kimahli Powell is also producer of b current's
rock.paper.sistahz festival and co-producer of Buddies
in Bad Times' queer and intercultural art sexy. African
Canadian playwright Djanet Sears, the artistic director of
the AfriCanadian Playwrights Festival, dramaturged Kuna-
Rappahannock Monique Mojica's *Princess Pocahontas and the
Blue Spots*. Argentinian Canadian playwright and performer
Guillermo Verdecchia has been artistic director of Cahoots
Theatre Projects, has directed Filipino, First Nations, South
Asian, and Korean Canadian plays, and has collaborated as a
writer with Egyptian Canadian Marcus Youssef and Iranian
Canadian Camyar Chai. In attendance at a recent fu-GEN
Asian-Canadian Theatre company fundraiser were the artis-
tic directors of Native Earth, Obsidian Theatre, Modern
Times, Rasik Arts, Carlos Bulosan Theatre, Cahoots Theatre

Projects, and b current, the cutting-edge Caribbean/dub-theatre company, with its 'raiZin the sun' training wing.

The cooperation and cross-fertilisation that this type of exchange involves produce some fascinating outcomes. In 2007, Cahoots Theatre Projects, under their Chinese Filipino Canadian artistic director Jovanni Sy, co-produced with Modern Times Stage Company at Theatre Passe Muraille a play by Moroccan Canadian Ahmed Ghazali called *The Sheep and the Whale*. The play was translated by Quebecker Bobby Theodore, directed by Modern Times's Persian/Iranian Canadian artistic director Soheil Parsa, and featured a multi-racial cast. Set aboard a once-Russian, now-multinational freighter off the Strait of Gibraltar, the play mixed realism, surrealism, agit-prop, and the stylised, nightmarish repre-sentation of Aïd el-Kebir, the traditional Moroccan Festival of Sacrifice at which each family slaughters a sheep in memory of the prophet Ibrahim. On one level the production was a powerful indictment of an international monetary system that preys on the bodies of the displaced, diasporic, and desperate poor. On another level, however, as process and production the show embodied intercultural solidarities in Toronto and enacted a transference of embodied performative forms of cultural memory – in this case, trauma memory – through transformative movement. Like so many productions emer-ging from the city's intercultural performance ecology, the show constituted a suturing together of new, re-configured forms with the traditional performance forms that haunt them. Rejecting the atomising nostalgias of Canada's official multiculturalism, productions emerging from this perform-ance ecosystem, at their best, represent, enact, and transmit to diverse Toronto participant-audiences a genuinely transformative, border-crossing, intercultural memory, the visceral stitching together from below of a larger intercultural community in the city through performative acts of re-membering across real, acknowledged, and respected difference.

These theatre workers are cumulatively answering Himani Bannerji's call in *The Dark Side of the Nation* for the creation of solidarities, for the opening up, in the face of racism, Eurocentrism, ethnocentrism, and official multiculturalism, of 'a space for a broader community among us' (p. 158), a heterotopic space for alternate ordering, one that is neither static nor folkloric nor merely symbolic, in which new social identities and social formations are performatively forged out of the crucible of traditional performance forms, the technologies of contemporary theatrical practice, and the daily (hard) work of negotiating across real and acknowledged social and cultural difference.

Conclusion

I began this book with an account of the fraught, 'half-empty' histories of intercultural performance and its troubled discourses. I have ended with a heady, 'half-full' account of intercultural performance in one representative world city in which new, hybrid, and diasporic subjectivities are being performatively forged. In between I have aimed to broaden the historical and geographical scope of the inquiry, address some of the problems that have faced theorists of intercultural performance, track some developments in the field and the world since the 'interculture wars' of the 1980s and 1990s, and introduce some recent theoretical approaches that may enrich the inquiry and redress some historical imbalances.

But what haunts this inquiry and is never fully acknowledged as I move from pessimism to optimism is the historical and ongoing fact of real material differences in access, funding, and resources that prevent the emerging and newly vital practices of intercultural theatre that I have been describing from taking their full and proper places on the main stages of world cities, with formerly marginalised and colonised peoples in full control of their own representation and cultural negotiations and with their cultural integrity not static but intact. A similarly ongoing fact is that the *discourses* of intercultural performance, in this book and elsewhere, are dominated by theorists from western cultures who have privileged access to the means of production – including, in this case, scholarly texts, their distribution and use in classrooms, rehearsal halls, and elsewhere. It is only when the migrant, diasporic, and Indigenous peoples of the world gain more control over the funding, spaces, and processes of production that the evolving rich and fertile ecologies of intercultural performance and its critical discourses can generate a body of work that might, in the words of Montreal's intercultural Teesri Duniya Theatre, 'change the world, one play at a time'.

further reading

I have listed below everything that I have cited, and a little more. The key texts addressing intercultural or cross-cultural performance are Christopher Balme's *Decolonizing the Stage*, Rustom Bharucha's *Theatre and the World* and *The Politics of Cultural Practice*, Erika Fischer-Lichte et al.'s *The Dramatic Touch of Difference*, Julie Holledge and Joanne Tompkins's *Women's Intercultural Performance*, Jacqueline Lo and Helen Gilbert's 'Toward a Topography of Cross-Cultural Theatre Praxis', Bonnie Marranca and Gautam Dasgupta's *Interculturalism and Performance*, and Patrice Pavis's *Theatre at the Crossroads of Culture* and *The Intercultural Performance Reader*.

On performance studies, see Henry Bial's *The Performance Studies Reader* and Richard Schechner's *Performance Studies: An Introduction* (which also has a good section on 'Global and Intercultural Performance').

Critical multiculturalism studies sports many readers, including David Theo Goldberg's *Multiculturalism:*

A Critical Reader; Barry Kanpol and Peter McLaren's *Critical Multiculturalism*, which emerges from the burgeoning field of critical pedagogy; and Amy Gutman's *Multiculturalism*, which includes Charles Taylor's influential article 'The Politics of Recognition'. The field also boasts many outstanding monographs, chief among which I would rank Himani Bannerji's *The Dark Side of the Nation* and Sneja Gunew's *Haunted Nations* – though Bannerji, at least, might identify her work as critical of multiculturalism rather than as critical multiculturalism studies.

Among the workhorses of critical race theory and critical whiteness studies are Richard Delgado and Jean Stefancic, who together wrote the useful primer *Critical Race Theory: An Introduction* and edited the two massive volumes *Critical Race Theory: The Cutting Edge* and *Critical Whiteness Studies: Looking Behind the Mirror*. Another anthology, *Critical Race Theory: The Key Writings That Formed the Movement*, is edited by Kimberlé Crenshawe et al. from a primarily legal perspective. Ruth Frankenberg and Mike Hill, respectively, edited *Displacing Whiteness* and *Whiteness: A Critical Reader*, and key studies in the field are Richard Dyer's classic *White*; Julian B. Carter's *The Heart of Whiteness*, which demonstrates the white heterosexual construction of the 'normal'; and George Lipsitz's brilliant *The Possessive Investment in Whiteness*, whose subtitle, 'How White People Profit from Identity Politics', explains it all.

Diaspora studies is well represented by Jana Evans Braziel and Anita Mannur's *Theorizing Diaspora*, and in application to the study of intercultural performance by

Yan Haiping's *Other Transnationals*, a special issue of the journal *Modern Drama*. Critical cosmopolitanism can be accessed in terms of performance by way of Helen Gilbert and Jacqueline Lo's *Performance and Cosmopolitics*, which has a good bibliography for those who want to explore the field.

Abu-Laban, Yasmeen, and Christina Gabriel. *Selling Diversity: Immigration, Multiculturalism, Employment Equity, and Globalization.* Peterborough, ON: Broadview, 2002.

Appiah, Kwame Anthony. 'Cosmopolitan Reading.' *Cosmopolitan Geographies: Thinking and Feeling beyond the Nation.* Ed. Vinay Dharwadker. New York: Routledge, 2001. 197–227.

Artaud, Antonin. 'On the Balinese Theater.' *The Theatre and Its Double.* Trans. Mary Caroline Richards. New York: Grove, 1958. 53–67.

Balme, Christopher. 'Between Separation and Integration: Intercultural Strategies in Contemporary Maori Theatre.' *The Intercultural Performance Reader.* Ed. Patrice Pavis. London: Routledge, 1996. 179–87.

————. *Decolonizing the Stage: Theatrical Syncretism and Post-Colonial Drama.* Oxford: Clarendon, 1999.

Bannerji, Himani. *The Dark Side of the Nation.* Toronto: Canadian Scholars' Press, 2000.

Barba, Eugenio, and Nicola Savarese. *A Dictionary of Theatre Anthropology: The Secret Art of the Performer.* Trans. Richard Fowler. London: Routledge, 1991.

Barker, Clive. 'The Possibilities and Politics of Intercultural Penetration and Exchange.' *The Intercultural Performance Reader.* Ed. Patrice Pavis. London: Routledge, 1996. 247–56.

Bhabha, Homi K. *The Location of Culture.* London: Routledge, 1994.

Bharucha, Rustom. *Theatre and the World: Performance and the Politics of Culture.* London: Routledge, 1993.

————. *The Politics of Cultural Practice: Thinking Through Theatre in an Age of Globalization.* Hanover, NH: Wesleyan UP, 2000.

Bial, Henry, ed. *The Performance Studies Reader.* New York: Routledge, 2004.

Brandon, James R. 'Contemporary Japanese Theatre: Interculturalism and Intraculturalism.' *The Dramatic Touch of Difference: Theatre, Own and Foreign*. Ed. Erika Fischer-Lichte, Josephine Riley, and Michael Gissenwehrer. Tübingen, Germany: Gunter Narr, 1990. 89–97.

Braziel, Jana Evans, and Anita Mannur, eds. *Theorizing Diaspora*. Oxford: Blackwell, 2003.

Brecht, Bertolt. 'Alienation Effects in Chinese Acting.' *Brecht on Theatre*. Ed. and trans. John Willett. New York: Hill and Wang, 1964. 91–9.

Brewer, Mary F. *Staging Whiteness*. Middletown, CT: Wesleyan UP, 2005.

Brook, Peter. *The Empty Space* [1968]. Harmondsworth, UK: Penguin, 1979.

———. *The Shifting Point: Theatre, Film, Opera 1946–1987*. New York: Harper & Row, 1987.

Butler, Judith. 'Performative Acts and Gender Constitution: An Essay on Phenomenology and Feminist Theory.' *Theatre Journal* 40.4 (1988): 519–31.

Carlson, Marvin. 'Peter Brook's "The Mahabharata" and Ariane Mnouchkine's "L'Indiade" as Examples of Contemporary Cross-Cultural Theatre.' *The Dramatic Touch of Difference: Theatre, Own and Foreign*. Ed. Erika Fischer-Lichte, Josephine Riley, and Michael Gissenwehrer. Tübingen, Germany: Gunter Narr, 1990. 49–56.

———. 'Brook and Mnouchkine: Passages to India?' *The Intercultural Performance Reader*. Ed. Patrice Pavis. London: Routledge, 1996. 79–92.

Carter, Jill. 'Writing, Righting, "Riting": *The Scrubbing Project* Re-members a New "Nation" and Reconfigures Ancient Ties.' *alt.theatre: cultural diversity and the stage* 4.4 (2006): 13–17.

Carter, Julian B. *The Heart of Whiteness: Normal Sexuality and Race in America, 1880–1940*. Durham, NC: Duke UP, 2007.

Chang, Dongshin. 'Intercultural Performance.' *Encyclopedia of Case Study Research*. Ed. Albert J. Mills, Gabrielle Durepos, and Elden Wiebe. Thousand Oaks, CA: Sage, 2010. 481–84.

Chaudhuri, Una. 'The Future of the Hyphen: Interculturalism, Textuality, and the Difference Within.' *Interculturalism and Performance: Writings from PAJ.* Ed. Bonnie Marranca and Gautam Dasgupta. New York: PAJ, 1991. 192–207.

Chin, Daryl. 'Interculturalism, Postmodernism, Pluralism.' *Interculturalism and Performance: Writings from PAJ.* Ed. Bonnie Marranca and Gautam Dasgupta. New York: PAJ, 1991. 83–95.

Conquergood, Dwight. 'Performance Studies: Interventions and Radical Research.' *The Drama Review* 46.2 (2002): 145–56.

Crenshaw, Kimberlé, Neil Gotanda, Gary Peller, and Kendall Thomas, eds. *Critical Race Theory: The Key Writings That Formed the Movement.* New York: New Press, 1995.

Crow, Brian. 'Issues in Multicultural Theatre: Birmingham Rep and Its Audiences.' *Staging New Britain: Aspects of Black and South Asian British Theatrical Practice.* Ed. Geoffrey V. Davis and Anne Fuchs. Brussels: PIE Peter Lang, 2006. 107–26.

Davis, Geoffrey V., and Anne Fuchs, eds. *Staging New Britain: Aspects of Black and South Asian British Theatrical Practice.* Brussels: PIE Peter Lang, 2006.

Delgado, Richard, and Jean Stefancic, eds. *Critical White Studies: Looking Behind the Mirror.* Philadelphia, PA: Temple UP, 1997.

———, eds. *Critical Race Theory: The Cutting Edge.* 2nd ed. Philadelphia, PA: Temple UP, 2000.

———. *Critical Race Theory: An Introduction.* New York: New York UP, 2001.

Ding Yangzhong. 'On the Insatiable Appetite and Longevity of Theatre.' *The Dramatic Touch of Difference: Theatre, Own and Foreign.* Ed. Erika Fischer-Lichte, Josephine Riley, and Michael Gissenwehrer. Tübingen, Germany: Gunter Narr, 1990. 169–77.

Dionne, Craig, and Parmita Kapadia, eds. *Native Shakespeares: Indigenous Appropriations on a Global Stage.* Aldershot, UK: Ashgate, 2008.

Dyer, Richard. *White.* London: Routledge, 1997.

Fanon, Frantz. *Black Skin, White Masks.* Trans. Charles Lan Markmann. New York: Grove, 1967.

Fiebach, Joachim. 'Wole Soyinka and Heiner Müller: Different Cultural Contexts, Similar Approaches.' *The Dramatic Touch of Difference:*

Theatre, Own and Foreign. Ed. Erika Fischer-Lichte, Josephine Riley, and Michael Gissenwehrer. Tübingen, Germany: Gunter Narr, 1990. 263–73.

Fischer-Lichte, Erika. 'Staging the Foreign as Cultural Transformation.' *The Dramatic Touch of Difference: Theatre, Own and Foreign*. Ed. Erika Fischer-Lichte, Josephine Riley, and Michael Gissenwehrer. Tübingen, Germany: Gunter Narr, 1990. 277–87.

———. 'Theatre, Own and Foreign. The Intercultural Trend in Contemporary Theatre.' *The Dramatic Touch of Difference: Theatre, Own and Foreign*. Ed. Erika Fischer-Lichte, Josephine Riley, and Michael Gissenwehrer. Tübingen, Germany: Gunter Narr, 1990. 11–19.

———. 'Interculturalism in Contemporary Theatre.' *The Intercultural Performance Reader*. Ed. Patrice Pavis. London: Routledge, 1996. 27–40.

Fischer-Lichte, Erika, Josephine Riley, and Michael Gissenwehrer, eds. *The Dramatic Touch of Difference: Theatre, Own and Foreign*. Tübingen, Germany: Gunter Narr, 1990.

Frankenberg, Ruth, ed. *Displacing Whiteness: Essays in Social and Cultural Criticism*. Durham, NC: Duke UP, 1997.

Gainor, J. Ellen, ed. *Imperialism and Theatre: Essays on World Theatre, Drama and Performance 1795–1995*. London: Routledge, 1995.

Gilbert, Helen. 'Black and White and Re(a)d All Over Again: Indigenous Minstrelsy in Contemporary Canadian and Australian Theatre.' *Theatre Journal* 55 (2003): 679–98.

Gilbert, Helen, and Jacqueline Lo. *Performance and Cosmopolitics: Cross-Cultural Transactions in Australia*. Houndmills, UK: Palgrave Macmillan, 2007.

Gilroy, Paul. *The Black Atlantic: Modernity and Double Consciousness*. Cambridge, MA: Harvard UP, 1993.

Goldberg, David Theo, ed. *Multiculturalism: A Critical Reader*. Oxford: Blackwell, 1994.

Goodman, Lizbeth, and Jane de Gay, eds. *The Routledge Reader in Politics and Performance*. London: Routledge, 2000.

Grotowski, Jerzy. 'Performer.' *The Grotowski Sourcebook*. Ed. Lisa Wolford and Richard Schechner. London: Routledge, 1997. 376–80.

Gunew, Sneja. *Haunted Nations: The Colonial Dimensions of Multiculturalisms*. London: Routledge, 2004.

Gutman, Amy, ed. *Multiculturalism: The Politics of Recognition*. Princeton, NJ: Princeton UP, 1994.

Hetherington, Kevin. *The Badlands of Modernity: Heterotopia and Social Ordering*. London: Routledge, 1997.

Hill, Mike, ed. *Whiteness: A Critical Reader*. New York: New York UP, 1997.

Holledge, Julie, and Joanne Tompkins. *Women's Intercultural Performance*. London: Routledge, 2000.

Hunter, Mead. 'Interculturalism and American Music.' *Interculturalism and Performance: Writings from PAJ*. Ed. Bonnie Marranca and Gautam Dasgupta. New York: PAJ, 1991. 291–307.

JanMohamed, Abdul R., and David Lloyd, eds. *The Nature and Context of Minority Discourse*. New York: Oxford UP, 1991.

Kanpol, Barry, and Peter McLaren, eds. *Critical Multiculturalism: Uncommon Voices in a Common Struggle*. Westport, CT: Bergin & Garvey, 1995.

Kant, Immanuel. *Political Writings*. Ed. H. Reiss. 2nd ed. Cambridge: Polity, 1990.

Knowles, Ric. 'Multicultural Text, Intercultural Performance: Performing Intercultural Toronto.' *Performance and the City*. Ed. D. J. Hopkins, Shelley Orr, and Kim Solga. Basingstoke, UK: Palgrave Macmillan, 2009. 73–91.

Lane, Jill. 'Black/face Publics: The Social Bodies of *Fraternidad*.' *Critical Theory and Performance*. Ed. Janelle G. Reinelt and Joseph R. Roach. 2nd ed. Ann Arbor: U of Michigan P, 2007. 141–55.

Laronde, Sandra. Interview with the author. 9 August 2006. Red Sky Performance office, Toronto.

Lei, Daphne. 'Virtual Chinatown and New Racial Formation: Performance of Cantonese Opera in the Bay Area.' *Critical Theory and Performance*. Ed. Janelle G. Reinelt and Joseph R. Roach. 2nd ed. Ann Arbor: U of Michigan P, 2007. 156–72.

Lipsitz, George. *The Possessive Investment in Whiteness: How White People Profit from Identity Politics*. Philadelphia, PA: Temple UP, 1998.

Lo, Jacqueline, and Helen Gilbert. 'Toward a Topography of Cross-Cultural Theatre Praxis.' *The Drama Review* 46.3 (2002): 31–53.

Marranca, Bonnie, and Gautam Dasgupta, eds. *Interculturalism and Performance: Writings from PAJ*. New York: PAJ, 1991.

Mojica, Monique. 'Of Borders, Identity, and Cultural Icons: A Rant.' *Canadian Theatre Review* 125 (2006): 35–40.

Mojica, Monique. 'Stories from the Body: Blood Memory and Organic Texts.' *alt.theatre: cultural diversity and the stage* 4.2–3 (2006): 16–20.

Murray, Christopher. 'Introduction to Part Three: Theorizing and Playing: Intercultural Perspectives.' *The Routledge Reader in Politics and Performance*. Ed. Lizbeth Goodman and Jane de Gay. London: Routledge, 2000. 85–9.

Nolan, Yvette. Interview with the author. 29 June 2006. Native Earth Performing Arts office, Distillery District, Toronto.

Ngugi wa Thiong'o. *Decolonising the Mind: The Politics of Language in African Literature*. London: Currey, 1986.

Pavis, Patrice. 'Interculturalism in Contemporary Mise en Scène: The Image of India in "The Mahabharata" and the "Indiade".' *The Dramatic Touch of Difference: Theatre, Own and Foreign*. Ed. Erika Fischer-Lichte, Josephine Riley, and Michael Gissenwehrer. Tübingen, Germany: Gunter Narr, 1990. 57–71.

———. *Theatre at the Crossroads of Culture*. Trans. Loren Kruger. London: Routledge, 1992.

———, ed. *The Intercultural Performance Reader*. London: Routledge, 1996.

Phelan, Peggy. 'Introduction: The Ends of Performance.' *The Ends of Performance*. Ed. Peggy Phelan and Jill Lane. New York: New York UP, 1998. 1–19.

Potiki, Roma. '"It Is Political If It Can Be Passed On": An Interview with Roma Potiki.' By Christopher Balme. *The Intercultural Performance Reader*. Ed. Patrice Pavis. London: Routledge, 1996. 172–8.

Qadeer, Mohammed, and Sandeep Kumar. 'Ethnic Enclaves and Social Cohesion.' *Our Diverse Cities: Challenges and Opportunities*. Spec. iss. of *Canadian Journal of Urban Research* 15.2 (Supplement, 2006): 1–17.

Reinelt, Janelle G., and Joseph R. Roach, eds. *Critical Theory and Performance*. 2nd ed. Ann Arbor: U of Michigan P, 2007.

Roach, Joseph R. 'Introduction [to Cultural Studies].' *Critical Theory and Performance*. [1st ed]. Ed. Janelle G. Reinelt and Joseph R. Roach. Ann Arbor: U of Michigan P, 1992.

———. *Cities of the Dead: Circum-Atlantic Performance*. New York: Columbia UP, 1996.

Rotimi, Ola. 'Much Ado about Brecht.' *The Dramatic Touch of Difference: Theatre, Own and Foreign*. Ed. Erika Fischer-Lichte, Josephine Riley, and Michael Gissenwehrer. Tübingen, Germany: Gunter Narr, 1990. 253–61.

Said, Edward. *Orientalism*. New York: Pantheon, 1978.

Schechner, Richard. *The End of Humanism: Writings on Performance*. New York: PAJ, 1982.

———. *Performance Theory*. Rev. ed. London: Routledge, 1988.

———. 'Interculturalism and the Culture of Choice.' *The Intercultural Performance Reader*. Ed. Patrice Pavis. London: Routledge, 1996. 41–50.

———. *Performance Studies: An Introduction*. London: Routledge, 2002.

Schechner, Richard, and Mady Schuman, eds. *Ritual, Play, and Performance: Readings in the Social Sciences/Theatre*. New York: Continuum, 1976.

Sears, Djanet. *Harlem Duet*. Winnipeg, MB: Scirocco, 1997.

Shohat, Ella, and Robert Stam. *Unthinking Eurocentrism: Multiculturalism and the Media*. London: Routledge, 1994.

Taylor, Charles. 'The Politics of Recognition.' *Multiculturalism: The Politics of Recognition*. Ed. Amy Gutman. Princeton, NJ: Princeton UP, 1994. 25–74.

Teesri Duniya Theatre. Mission and Activities. 4 July 2009 <http://teesriduniyatheatre.com/mission.html>.

Todd, Rebecca. 'Enlivening the Land: Red Sky's Integrative Approach.' *the dance current* March 2003: 22–5.

Turner, Victor. *The Anthropology of Performance*. New York: PAJ, 1987.

Williams, Gary Jay. 'Interculturalism, Hybridity, Tourism: The Performing World on New Terms.' *Theatre Histories: An Introduction*. Ed. Phillip B. Zarrilli, Bruce McConachie, Gary Jay Williams, and Carol Fisher Sorgenfrei. New York: Routledge, 2006. 485–519.

Wirth, Andrzej. 'Interculturalism and Iconophilia in the New Theatre.' *Interculturalism and Performance: Writings from PAJ*. Ed. Bonnie Marranca and Gautam Dasgupta. New York: PAJ, 1991. 281–90.

Yan Haiping, ed. *Other Transnationals: Asian Diaspora in Performance*. Spec. iss. of *Modern Drama* 48.2 (2005).

———. 'Other Transnationals: An Introductory Essay.' *Other Transnationals: Asian Diaspora in Performance*. Spec. iss. of *Modern Drama* 48.2 (2005): 225–48.

Zarrilli, Phillip B. 'For Whom Is the King a King? Issues of Intercultural Production, Perception, and Reception in a *Kathakali King Lear*.' *Critical Theory and Performance*. Ed. Janelle G. Reinelt and Joseph R. Roach. 2nd ed. Ann Arbor: U of Michigan P, 2007. 108–33.

Zarrilli, Phillip B., Bruce McConachie, Gary Jay Williams, and Carol Fisher Sorgenfrei. *Theatre Histories: An Introduction*. New York: Routledge, 2006.

index